THE GOD
WHO SAYS YES

THE GOD
WHO SAYS YES

WALTER SCRAGG

REVIEW AND HERALD PUBLISHING ASSOCIATION
Washington, DC 20039-0555
Hagerstown, MD 21740

This book was
Edited by Gerald Wheeler
Designed by Richard Steadham
Cover photos by The Genesis Project
Type set: 11/12 Zapf

Printed in U.S.A.

Library of Congress Cataloging in Publication Data

Scragg, Walter R. L., 1925-
    The God who says yes.

    1. Bible. N.T. Luke—Criticism, interpretation,
etc. I. Title.
BS2595.2.S37   1987   226'.406   86-27991
ISBN 0-8280-0376-9

"The Son of God, Christ Jesus, proclaimed among you by us . . . , was never a blend of Yes and No. With him it was, and is, Yes. He is the Yes pronounced upon God's promises, every one of them."

—2 Cor. 1:19, 20, NEB

Contents

Introduction

How should we think of Luke? He gave to future generations of Christians one of the four inspired Gospels and wrote the only contemporary history of the first century church. Is he just a clone of the other Gospel authors? Do we learn little more from him than we might gather from Matthew, Mark, or John?

We owe this remarkable man an infinite debt. Under the inspiration of the Holy Spirit, he provided us information about Jesus Christ quite different from that given by the other three Gospel writers. Even when he used the same stories, he put them together in his own style. He had a special vision he wanted to share about Jesus Christ and the God who sent Him among us.

Luke's view of Jesus sets Luke apart as a theologian of extraordinary skill. You may be certain that he thought through carefully what he wanted to say about Jesus and the infant church. Take any section of his Gospel and you will discern a pattern being developed. He tells us that he has written a "connected narrative" giving "authentic knowledge" (Luke 1:3, 4, NEB).

Thus he invites us to look for connections, to see purpose and plan. He guides us on a journey through a realm of spiritual insights. But we must never think that what he writes has any element of fiction or fantasy. Luke "has gone over the whole course of these events in detail" (verse 3, NEB).

You may therefore come to his Gospel in different ways. Mine it for historical truth about Jesus, and you will unearth treasure. Look for connections between events, perhaps widely separated by time and place, and you will find them.

The reader may rightly picture Luke as an inquisitive and thorough seeker after facts about Jesus. He had access to the "original eyewitnesses" (verse 2, NEB). Mark had already written his Gospel. Luke either knew Mark's work or shared a common source from which both drew. Matthew, along with Luke, tapped into material that Mark either did not have or chose not to use. At times it seems Luke and John both plucked from the great store of information about Jesus (see John 21:25) and selected the same event.

But that does not tell the whole story. Under the Spirit's eye, from Luke's research, come stories he alone recorded. Having observed the leading of the Spirit in so many of the persons he features, Luke looked to the Spirit for the same guidance. The Gospel writer knew the power of prayer and spoke frequently of the presence of the holy angels. He observed how God worked out His plans through individual lives, and felt himself under the same Guiding Hand.

Luke made stories interesting. In fact, he loved a good story. For this reason his book contains many stories about Jesus not found in the other Gospels. He uses them with telling effect as he portrays the purpose and plan God had set in motion.

An educated convert from the Gentile world, Luke employed the forms of writing common to his day. The Greeks often set stories about their heroes in the form of a journey. Luke does so in both his Gospel and the Acts.

As a physician he experienced all too often the frailty that surrounded him. Sickness brought rich and poor, powerful and weak, educated and ignorant, Roman and

Jew, to the same basic need of healing and wholeness. In a world where any serious illness almost certainly meant death, he knew how desperately inadequate his own efforts must be.

It should come as no surprise therefore that Luke, of all the Gospel writers, most urgently stresses the common humanity of all people. The world lies at death's door and needs a Healer, a Saviour. The common lot that leads all through sickness and suffering to death models a view of Jesus that belongs especially to Luke. All are equal before God, and all need salvation. God wants to give that salvation. Any individual who obstructs God in His quest must answer for it. And anyone who fails to follow the divine pattern of compassion for the weak also must face judgment.

Luke presents God as Saviour of the world. Because He seeks to save all, He is the God who says yes to all. Not that all say yes to His saving action in Jesus Christ. But His yes reaches the rich, the powerful, and the educated, and above all, the poor and the ordinary people.

God sustains the Son of man, who came to seek and save the lost. He rejects systems that exclude people from Him or that create categories. In Luke, God makes His yes loud and clear. He wants you in His kingdom.

The Gospel writer stresses the continuity between the Son of man, who saved and healed on earth, and the Son of God, who directs His saving and healing power from the right hand of the throne of the universe. Thus he reassures us that we may share the same saving and healing power witnessed so long ago.

Begin With
the Spirit

Luke 1:1-2:52

Luke loves to chronicle the acts of the Spirit. None of God's plans for mankind can begin without the Spirit. Warmed by the Holy Wind, the cocoon of humility and devotion unfolds with the beautiful wings of salvation.

Every worthwhile departure begins with the Spirit. Like an airport traffic controller, the Spirit directs the saving acts of God as He works out God's plan.

Benefiting From the Spirit

1. *The Spirit works best among humble, devoted people—ordinary people without pretensions or self-importance.*

Zacharias did not belong to the group that served all the time at the Temple. He had come to Jerusalem according to a roster (Luke 1:5, 8) that gave each of the estimated 43,000 active priests turns in Temple duty.

Our devotion to God's will gives Him a starting point. Luke called Zacharias and Elisabeth upright, devout, blameless, obedient to "all the commandments and ordinances of the Lord" (verse 6, NEB).[1] Such people suit God's purposes. He can trust them with a miracle. As the yes of their devotion meets the yes of His grace, He can in fact "move mountains."

The Spirit found Zacharias and Elisabeth rather than their finding the Spirit. We know nothing of the couple's prayer until the angel appeared beside the altar (verses

11-13). Character, rather than prayers, qualifies one for the Spirit's action.

"The position of the angel was an indication of favor, but Zacharias took no note of this. For many years he had prayed for the coming of the Redeemer; now heaven had sent its messenger to announce that these prayers were about to be answered; but the mercy of God seemed too great for him to credit. He was filled with fear and self-condemnation."[2]

˙ The catalyst for the descent of the Spirit is a character that demonstrates faith (see verse 6). The free Spirit moves as the wind in His quest for those through whom He may do great things.

2. *The filling of the Spirit marks God's initiatives among humanity.*

What did Luke mean by being filled with the Spirit? In the name of the Spirit all kinds of bizarre and faith-destroying beliefs have flourished. Armies have marched to slaughter claiming the Spirit. Cults have led people to death in the name of the Spirit.

The Spirit filled John (verse 15). From the moment of birth he lived out God's purpose. His miracle birth witnessed to the world that something great would soon happen. John testified, at first simply by his existence, then by his preaching, that God was doing something marvelous.

The Spirit filled Zacharias, and he prophesied (verse 67). From the filling of the Spirit, something great will happen in the plan of God. When the Spirit filled Jesus (Luke 4:1), the tempter met defeat in the wilderness. The Spirit armed Jesus with power to begin His ministry (verse 14). In the same way the early Christians, filled with the Spirit, spilled out into the streets of Jerusalem and began the spread of the gospel (Acts 2:4).

In the last days, the filling of the Spirit will signal the falling of the latter rain and the beginning of the end. As with the time of Zacharias' prophecy and the tongues of fire on the day of Pentecost, the moment of filling comes at the Spirit's discretion. We, like John's parents, wait in meekness and consecration for the Spirit to move.

If you are waiting for the latter rain, depend totally on Christ's righteousness. Shun self-importance and self-righteousness. Accept the weakness of humanity and call in prayer for the Almighty to give strength.

3. *The Spirit dwells with all God's people.*

The Spirit goes between you and the world, blessing and enlarging your witness. He gives you His gifts, nurtures in you His fruits. At no point do you live without the Spirit. He convicts, guides, and instructs all the way to heaven.

To plead "Lord, fill me with Your Spirit" is a most appropriate prayer. It teaches us to submit, to study God's purposes, to seek His leading. But that was not the way in which Luke used the concept *filling of the Spirit.* For him, such a filling marked a significant new departure in God's purposes. With these words the history of salvation took a new direction or a new impetus.

4. *The Spirit's work points us toward the future.*

"Elisabeth will bear you a son.... He will be great in the eyes of the Lord." "All generations will count me blessed." "You will be the Lord's forerunner" (Luke 1:13, 15, 48, 76, NEB).

The Holy Spirit works for us with the future in view because He knows God's mind. Through Him the purposes of God create spiritual good out of our disordered lives (Rom. 8:28). He knows how the promises can be fulfilled for you.

Alvin Toffler in his book *Future Shock* sought to prepare us for what would most likely happen in the coming decades. But that author had no control over his predictions. The Spirit—God's futurologist—knows the future and goes with us into it.

Luke clearly understood the role of the Spirit. Without Him John the Baptist had no future within God's purposes. Without Him the Holy Child of promise could never appear. Without Him the church cannot fulfill God's will. And without Him we will never live victoriously for our Lord.

Because we do not know what the future holds, He is our comforter. Because we cannot direct our own paths in righteousness, He is our guide. Because we cannot of ourselves discern truth, He is our teacher. Because we cannot see God, He is the revealer. And because we cannot know how best to witness, He is the giver of gifts.

Jewels of Faith

If you visit the Tower of London and examine the crown jewels of the British royal family, your eyes will go naturally to certain gems. They attract your attention above all the others, beautiful though the rest are. In Luke's two-volume work, special jewels of faith and belief adorn the diadem of truth. They begin to sparkle in the first chapters of the Gospel.

Prayer. As the story begins, the multitude at the Temple is praying (Luke 1:10). At the opening of the book of Acts, the 120 who form the first Christian congregation also pray (Acts 1:14, 15). If the filling of the Spirit marks a new initiative from God, prayer establishes the spiritual climate in which such an initiative may occur.

Luke's books urge us to intercessory prayer. Jesus prayed frequently. The early church prayed. In intercessory prayer we will discover the key to victorious living and to witnessing power.

Angels. W. A. Spicer, the General Conference president who wrote *The Hand That Intervenes*, would have been at home in the world of Luke. An angel appears as the Gospel begins (Luke 1:11). To angels God gives the responsibility of speaking directly with humans. The angel discusses Zacharias's plight with him (verse 13). The angel answers the perplexed Mary (verses 28-38). Another angel helps Peter to get out of prison (Acts 12:7-11).

Women. In that world, whether Roman, Greek, or Hebrew, women had no prominent religious, social, or cultural role to play. In contrast Luke makes them the mouthpiece of the Spirit as they praise God in chapter 1. He will continue this emphasis throughout his Gospel. Did Luke send his Gospel into a Christian community where women held considerable positions in the affairs of the church? It would appear so.

Humble people. While Matthew took care to record the visit of the Wise Men to the infant Jesus, Luke focused on the innkeeper (inferred in Luke 2:7) and the shepherds (verses 8-18). The One about whom the Pharisees scoffed, "This man receiveth sinners" (Luke 15:2), received them first as a babe in a manger (Luke 2:7). Shepherds, because they associated with animals and their excreta, had little hope for ritual cleanliness in the then current view of the Law of Moses. With God the least likely may become the greatest in faith and witness, such is the power of His yes.

Witness. The songs and psalms pouring from the lips of the Spirit-filled have more than one function. Not only did Luke record them to show how these amazed and exultant servants of God reacted to such marvelous events, but they also serve as witnessing models. Each of them ties directly with Old Testament prophecies and promises. Like the speeches of Paul and Peter in Acts, Luke intended that those who wish to witness to their Lord would find models here.

God Fulfills His Promise

Adventist Christians will feel at home with Luke. Luke tied together prophecy and fulfillment with witnessing.

"See," he says, "this event is a fulfillment of prophecy. Let that be known so that Christ may be believed and the sinner saved."

Was Luke a theologian or a historian? Enough books to fill a shelf have sought an answer to this question. Perhaps the best answer would be that he wrote history with a theological perspective. In other words, his theology fits into a historical framework.

Luke created a sequence and arrayed his material to serve his purposes. Not that he did not follow events. Quite the contrary. One of the marks of his writing was his love for detail and incident.

History records the saving acts of God. Salvation enters real time, real history. It happens on earth, to ordinary people. Those who trust in God share in the history of salvation.

By the time Luke penned his Gospel, about three decades had passed since the Resurrection. To many, Jesus remained an enigma. Was He God masquerading as man? Was He so much a spirit that He left no footprints, as the Gnostics asserted? Was He a man whom God specially singled out? Or was He a man taken over by God, controlled by God? Reading the Gospel, you can discern between the lines the questions Luke had to answer.

While Luke did not hesitate to name Augustus and Quirinius at the beginning of chapter 2, his concern was for authentic knowledge about Jesus Christ, not precise historical accuracy. Those who quibble over historical details miss the point: Jesus is really man. Not too many years ago He lived, ministered, and died in the real world of Palestine. In fact, His life and career began in the reign of Augustus and continued into the reign of Tiberius (Luke 3:1).

Luke understood the importance of history. He charted a Man and a movement as they fulfill prophecy. Of course, he was not alone in this. The whole New

Testament sees the chief significance of a historical event in its fulfillment of prophecy. Thus God writes the history of salvation.

The Reactions of Faith

How do you react to the story of Jesus' birth? Luke both records how we should respond and how people actually did. Those who, like Zacharias, doubt that God will carry out His long-promised purposes, need a lesson in faith (Luke 1:20-22). God will provide it for us as He did for the elderly priest.

Mary trembled at the thought of what God intended. Yet she submitted to His will. What if God asks unexpected things of us? Those of us who trust, like Mary, may wonder, but we will rejoice at the requests and then go and carry them out. She puts into our mouths words of response: "Behold the handmaid [servant] of the Lord; be it unto me according to thy word" (verse 38). With God nothing is impossible. All generations would call Mary blessed (verse 48). Her humble, submissive spirit teaches a lesson to every servant of the Lord.

When God asks of us the impossible, what will we do? When His commands confront us, will we turn them aside, or obey? Nothing could have prepared Mary for what the angel told her. How could anyone live with such a demand? Yet she magnified the Lord (verse 46), who accomplished great things through her.

When Jesus comes to us He brings joy (see Luke 1:14, 44, 58; 2:10). The shepherds speak for all who go to find Jesus Christ: "Let us now go . . . and see this thing which is come to pass, which the Lord hath made known unto us" (Luke 2:15). Later Jesus gave an invitation: "Come and see" (John 1:39). If we will only behold Him and trust Him, He will give eternal life.

We rejoice in the light,
And we echo the song
That comes down through the night
From the heavenly throng.
Aye! we shout to the lovely
Evangel they bring,
And we greet in His cradle
Our Savior and King![3]

The ordinary people of the world—shepherds without any claim to knowledge or authority—received the grandest news ever given. The humble circumstances of Jesus' birth did not faze them, despite the contrast with the blaze of angelic glory (Luke 2:9, 20).

If Acts stands number one in teaching divine models of witness for the church, Luke's Gospel presses hard on its heels. Did Theophilus and his fellow believers need stirring into action? Had they cooled in their ardor for Christ? Luke had a remedy. Look at how the eyewitnesses at the very start of his account reacted (verse 17). There's your model. Tell what you know God has done.

We find here no maverick child born to overthrow and disrupt the divine order. Joseph and Mary acted within the accepted practice for people of their situation (verses 21-24). She continued to ponder the meaning of all that had happened (verse 19), but she did not think the visit by the angel, nor the conception by the Holy Spirit, nor the events accompanying Jesus' birth so exceptional that she and Joseph might forgo the demands of the Law.

The second chapter of Luke reads like a testimony meeting. Witness after witness appeared to confirm the great event and its meaning.

Of Simeon, the Gospel writer says, "The same man was just and devout" (verse 25). To a man of this character the

Holy Ghost may promise that he would see "the Lord's Christ" (verse 26). The Spirit was "upon him" (verse 25). He came into the Temple "by the Spirit" (verse 27).

The angel had declared "good tidings . . . to all people" (verse 10). Now Simeon said that Jesus would "lighten the Gentiles" (verse 32). For too many Jews, such a universal message created difficulty. The Gentiles also had a problem that needed addressing: How could they relate to a Saviour who came from the proud and isolationist Jews?

Without a doubt Joseph and Mary played a significant role in the life of the young Jesus (verses 51, 52). Mary's thoughts dwelt on what others said of her Son. Both Joseph and Mary marveled "at those things" (verse 18). In the story of the trip to Jerusalem, Jesus obeyed His parents. His bout with the Temple theologians made Him neither conceited nor difficult (see verses 46-50). He continued to be subject to His parents (verse 51).

Luke gives no support to the fantastic and the fictitious tales that put Jesus in Arabia or China or other distant lands. Of both John and Jesus he said precisely the same: "The child grew, and waxed strong in spirit" (Luke 1:80; 2:40). John waited his destiny in the desert (Luke 1:80). Jesus received divine wisdom and grace (see Luke 2:52). Their homes provided both physical and spiritual nurture.

How should we relate to the miracle stories of Jesus' birth? Like Anna, the 84-year-old prophetess, give thanks for what God did (verses 36-38). Like her, witness to others about it. All that we have read so far matters only if we believe it as Anna did. It can help others only if we witness as she did.

The ordinary people of Judaea are Luke's heroes. God loved them, and they became His vessels to do His will. They submitted to Him and lived exemplary lives.

The Jews of that time believed that the Spirit had

departed from Israel. Now He returned to bring the astounding news of the Son of God born into humanity. These solid, honest, devout persons were God's most credible advocates. Their humble status precluded any human manipulator from pulling any strings.

Some 50 years after these events, Paul had occasion to reflect on the work of the Spirit. He numbered the gifts (1 Cor. 12:7-10), described the fruit (Gal. 5:22, 23). If you study Luke's writings carefully, you will discover that he saw the Spirit in the same light. Though he did not list them, he described the gifts in action. His ordinary people displayed the fruit in their lives.

Today we sometimes try to isolate the Spirit from His actions. Neither Luke nor Paul could do that. Luke especially has a practical message for us. The story of salvation begins with the Spirit. With the Spirit we live devout and righteous lives, and with the Spirit we witness to others of Jesus Christ.

---

[1] See *The Desire of Ages,* pp. 97, 98.

[2] *Ibid.*

[3] Josiah G. Holland, "There's a Song in the Air," *The Seventh-day Adventist Hymnal,* No. 120.

Help Comes for Ordinary People

Luke 3:1-4:37

How many names of world leaders (past or present) can you call to mind? Well, there's Reagan and Gorbachev, Roosevelt and Churchill, Truman, Kennedy, and . . . The list runs out after a short time. You probably know a greater number of names of ordinary people than those of the famous or wealthy.

If there's one message that comes through in Luke's Gospel, it is God's yes in Jesus to common man. He came looking for people who would accept the kingdom of heaven. Jesus really loved people. The Bible says He had compassion on them (Matt. 9:36), and He sought out anyone who showed an interest in God and His saving ways.

Not that Luke minded dropping the names of famous people. But usually he did that for a purpose. At the beginning of Luke 2 and again at the start of Luke 3 you will find lists of the famous of those days.

While Augustus and Tiberius hardly rank as household names in the late twentieth century, all who read Luke's scrolls would have been familiar with the names of these Romans. Who did not know the names of the emperors, especially the recent ones?

Some on Luke's lists wouldn't be so familiar. However, those who lived in the Middle East would have known the Herod family. Jews would recognize the names of the high priests (Luke 3:2).

The flavor of authenticity spices these passages. Luke's story isn't a make-believe. Like any good reporter, he can tell you where, when, why, and how it happened, and to whom.

Running Before the Lord

As the moment approached for Jesus to begin His ministry, that other miracle baby from chapter 1 also reached maturity. John strode out of the desert ready for the divine drama (Luke 3:2, 3).

He had something important for the people: baptism (verse 3). Unknown in the Old Testament, not practiced in the same way by other contemporary Jews or Gentiles, John demanded it of all who would show true repentance (verses 7-14).

Readers of the books of Moses will know that the Law commanded ritual washings (for example, Ex. 30:19-21). By the time of Jesus any convert to Judaism would wash and dip himself as a sign of his changed life.

How did baptism differ from ceremonial washings?

1. Baptism signified a changed, repentant lifestyle (Luke 3:8).

2. Immersion showed how the whole life must change (verses 11-14).

3. The one baptized declared his allegiance to the kingdom of God.

4. Baptism came to differ sharply from ritual washings. The repentant person did not baptize, or wash, himself. One whose life and authority came from God did the baptizing (see verse 7).

5. The ones baptized made ready a path, or way, for the Lord to do His work (see verses 4-6).

John did not have a distinct and separate ministry. The one God-willed event encircled both Jesus and John. From their births, through ministry and death, their witness heralded the one and same supreme event: the salvation of man.

Both Jesus and John discerned the tragedy of hypocrisy and formalism. Wickedness had filled the land like a loathsome tree (see verse 9). Now the preacher's word cut at the trunk of wickedness.

The fords that crossed the Jordan near Jericho carried a constant traffic of traders, priests, soldiers, and ordinary travelers. Standing by the river, animal skins tied around him, the preacher soon gathered a crowd. In the intensely religious atmosphere of that time, word spread quickly. From the surrounding towns and from Jerusalem, a good hard day's walk away, the people flocked to hear the preacher.

"For Luke, John's preaching is his most important act. He is the embodiment of Old Testament prophecy, which knows there can be no grace without judgment, no salvation without repentance, no forgiveness without a divine claim on the human will."[1]

No life can escape the demand to change. Crooked ways need straightening. Salvation lies only along the road of humble repentance, confession, and obedience.

In the last days John's Elijah message will sound once again. But the message that prepares for latter-day baptism will not fall gently on expectant ears. "God does not send messengers to flatter the sinner. He delivers no message of peace to lull the unsanctified into fatal security. He lays heavy burdens upon the conscience of the wrongdoer, and pierces the soul with arrows of conviction. The ministering angels present to him the fearful judgments of God to deepen the sense of need, and prompt the cry 'What must I do to be saved?' "[2]

As John wandered the rough trails and cliff tracks of the wilderness, the Lord showed him the lives of the people. Their leaders had fooled them. The desert of formalism must accept the rain of the Spirit and blossom as a rose. The hard places of persistent sin must crack under the hammer of the Word.

The ax of judgment (Luke 3:9) will fell the mightiest trunk of unrighteousness and hypocrisy. Ancient and modern Pharisees did and will experience the swinging thuds of judgment.

The coming of Jesus puts all in the crisis of judgment. The question What will you do with Jesus? lies at the heart of John's fiery preaching (see verse 16).

Luke reflects on the success of John with his hearers: "When they heard him [Jesus], all the people, including the tax-gatherers, praised God, for they had accepted John's baptism; but the Pharisees and lawyers, who refused his baptism, had rejected God's purpose for themselves" (Luke 7:29, 30, NEB).

What Repentance Means

Like the common people, the publicans, and the soldiers, we should ask, "What shall we do?" (Luke 3:10, 12, 14).

The repentant heart does not plead, Where or when shall I meditate, or What ritual shall I follow? It clamors to know What shall I do? God does not bring us to Him to confirm and bless our sinning ways. In the world of Hebrew thought, abstract notions or ideas cannot exist without appropriate action. No one can love without doing the deeds of love. No one can believe without confessing belief. And no one can pray without praying for right actions. No one can hope without living the life of that hope.

The viper generation (verse 7) failed to change their lives. But the ordinary people humbled themselves and accepted. Within the walls of Qumran, sectarian Jews demanded that all worldly possessions be shared with the community. John's converts, and later the church, did so from free choice.

The people responded to the coming judgment

through holy living. No other appropriate human response exists. Jesus, the mightier one (verse 16), would begin His ministry shortly. He waited, John said, grain shovel in hand, poised to toss the harvest high into the wind of the Spirit and winnow out the chaff (see verse 17). In a blaze of fierce heat the trash would vanish, and only the grain would remain.

In November 1985, Nevado del Ruiz, a volcano in Colombia, erupted. A wall of mud raced down the Langunilla River. The mud turned the town of Armero into a massive tomb. Rescuers found 13-year-old Omairo Sánchez mired neck deep in the mud. For 60 hours they tried to free her. But, buried deep beneath the mud, the arms of her dead aunt gripped her legs. Nothing would break the deadly embrace. Finally the trapped girl died of heart failure.

John declared, "Behold the Lamb of God, which taketh away the sin of the world" (John 1:29). Evil has embraced every soul. The landslide of sin threatens to bury us in eternal darkness. Only Jesus, the Lamb of God, can force the death lock of sin and free us to eternal life.

Come, Holy Spirit

Before Luke finished his two books, he explored a wide range of names for Jesus. Through them he tells us about the nature of God's Son. We have already heard Him called "the Son of God" (Luke 1:35), "an horn of salvation" (verse 69), "a Saviour" (Luke 2:11), "Christ the Lord" (verse 11), and "the Lord's Christ" (verse 26).

The story of Jesus' baptism, and the genealogy that follows, explore His nature and mission further. The baptism, as told by Luke, concentrates on the voice from heaven and the dove form the Spirit took (Luke 3:21, 22).

A knowledgeable Galilean, present that early autumn day in A.D. 27, might have remarked on the relationship between John and Jesus—they were cousins. Waist-deep in the water, John was baptizing a line of people snaking down into the river Jordan. Some may have reflected on John's prophecy of a Spirit baptism (verse 16). Nothing would have prepared the observer for what now happened.

Jesus came out of the water and immediately communed with God in prayer (verse 21). He was a praying Saviour. The early church was a praying church. A praying people should now await the descent of the Spirit.

While Jesus prostrated Himself in prayer, the Father sent the Holy Spirit. Why in the form of a dove? We do not know. The dove as a symbol of peace and of the Holy Spirit gathers force from that event rather than explaining it, though Noah found rest after the tumult of the Flood through the dove messenger (see Gen. 8:8-11). The scribes of Jesus' day referred to the Spirit's gentle voice, the *bath qol*, which had replaced the strong and certain voice of the prophets. But these understandings throw little light on the symbolism. All we really know is that with the baptism over, while Jesus was continuing in prayer, the Spirit came down in the form of a dove.

"The Saviour's glance seems to penetrate heaven as He pours out His soul in prayer. Well He knows how sin has hardened the hearts of men, and how difficult it will be for them to discern His mission, and accept the gift of salvation. . . . The heavens are opened, and upon the Saviour's head descends a dovelike form of purest light—fit emblem of Him, the meek and lowly One." [3]

> Come, Holy Spirit, heavenly Dove,
> With all Thy quickening powers;
> Kindle a flame of sacred love
> In these cold hearts of ours. [4]

Jesus' baptism showed both His identity with and His distinction from common humanity. He obeyed the will of God as we must. Yet, as the Lamb of God, He entered the water as the Sinless One who needed no repentance or cleansing.

John and Jesus

How should a Christian evaluate John? We have our Lord's own words about his greatness (Luke 7:28). Yet he remains somewhat of an enigma. We would like to know more about him.

Jesus saw Himself as carrying on a work begun by John (see Luke 9:18, 19; cf. Matt. 3:1, 2 with Matt. 4:17). We mistake the intent of Scripture if we regard the Baptist as a prelude to Jesus or if we look on him as isolated from Him. His message was neither second rate nor inferior. God integrated John into His plan. We cannot understand it fully without him.

"They [John and Jesus] summoned their hearers to immediate, unqualified, and self-denying obedience. Repentance was viewed by both as marking decisive preparation for the new age, as in fact identifying the boundary between old and new."[5]

John's movement was no small-time, hidden affair. A multitude (Luke 3:7) came out to be baptized by him. They obeyed his call in preparation for the mission of the Lord and the heralding of the kingdom.

Like John, God's messengers perceive the eternal and ultimate choice—either you prepare for the coming new age or you join the viper generation. We either go with God's plan or reject it, like the Pharisees rejected the counsel of God (Luke 7:30).

Perhaps you have puzzled at the reference to Jesus as "the Son of God." When did it happen? At Jesus' conception (Luke 1:32, 35)? At His baptism (Luke 3:22)? At His crucifixion (Acts 2:36; 3:13)? Timing gave no problem to Luke. Humanity may perceive this truth at different times or on different occasions. Christ's sonship never stands in question, however men relate to it. He is the Son of God from eternity, and His acts—and God's acts toward Him—show that sonship.

Not only is He the Son of God, acknowledged by God Himself, but He is also "the son of Adam, which was the son of God" (Luke 3:38)—acknowledged as truly human. Both Son and son, He forever carries His manhood with Him.

Luke linked Jesus to the covenant promises. Thus He is the son of Abraham (verse 34) and the son of David (verse 31). The gospel writer also tied Him in with Zerubbabel (verse 27), the priest of the restoration after the Exile. Many of the names Luke uses are unknowns, thus causing us to concentrate on the knowns. The genealogy carries its own prophecy of what Jesus will do.

Saying No to the Tempter

We have heard the voice of God. Now we hear the words of the tempter. In Eden Adam failed his destiny (Gen. 3:11, 12) and then felt compelled to hide from God (verse 8). Would this newly proclaimed Adam fare better?

Jesus accepted the body prepared for Him. "I come to do thy will, O God" (Heb. 10:9). Luke regarded the wilderness experience as part of God's will. "Full of the Holy Spirit, Jesus returned from the Jordan, and for forty days was led by the Spirit up and down the wilderness and tempted by the devil" (Luke 4:1, 2, NEB).

In the wilderness the Spirit had led the people of God (see Deut. 8:2). Now in the wilderness of life the Spirit leads us. We know only too well how we can fail Him. In contrast Jesus conquered every temptation. Filled by the Spirit (Luke 4:1, 18), He never wavered, but became the victorious Second Adam.

"According to Scripture, it is precisely those who are

called by God that are tempted because they are torn between their God, who will not set them free, and the world, whose suffering they share."[6]

Twenty centuries later Jesus still stands as our example. In the wilderness He met the tempter and refused him a place in His heart. We may share His victory as we too face the testing. His yes to the Word of God stands forever as a model and aids us as we give our yes to the will of God.

"Many claim that it was impossible for Christ to be overcome by temptation. Then He could not have been placed in Adam's position; He could not have gained the victory Adam failed to gain.... Our Saviour took humanity, with all its liabilities. He took the nature of man, with the possibility of yielding to temptation. We have nothing to bear which He has not endured."[7]

Sin and its perpetrator affronted the Son of God. But Jesus used no diplomacy. He met Satan head-on (verses 4, 12). Later He ordered Satan to get behind Him (verse 8). Never doubt the power of Satan. Such power must be met directly. The "roaring lion" will devour all who dally and dither in his presence.

Our Saviour refused a promise that did not fit the circumstances, while claiming one that did (verses 10-12). Through the Spirit, God guides those who need the Scriptures to sustain them. As Paul later put it, the Word of God is *the* weapon (Eph. 6:17), but the Spirit wields the sword.

Because Jesus won He may now rob the strong man (Satan) of his goods (his captives). (See Luke 11:21, 22.) Because of His victory we may come near to God (Heb. 4:15, 16).

The Sabbath and the Spirit

The Spirit does not create mystics or visionaries, though He may deal with mysteries and visions. The

Spirit filled Jesus so that He might fulfill God's purposes.

"The Spirit of the Lord is upon me" (Luke 4:18) carries a similar meaning to "the kingdom of God is come upon you" (Luke 11:20). The Spirit armed Jesus with power to perform miracles, and to teach with consummate authority.

Synagogues may have come into being during the Exile. They achieved a permanent role in Jewish life, even among the Jews who established colonies in distant lands. Without the synagogues, Judaism would never have survived the destruction of the Temple in A.D. 70.

When Jesus returned to Nazareth, He declared in the synagogue (verses 17-19) that in His ministry a year of jubilee had begun in which He would preach good news to the poor, heal the brokenhearted, and set the captives at liberty.

For the ancient year of jubilee (Lev. 25) the Lord provided food for His people, because the Jews were forbidden to plant and harvest. Those sold into bondage went free. Land rented or sold was returned to its rightful owner.

Hear the terms of Christ's jubilee: freedom from the bondage of sin, fruits of righteousness in the life, a place in the kingdom of heaven. The year of heavenly jubilee began that day in Nazareth. Each new day marks another in the continuing jubilee experience of God's people.

But some prefer it otherwise. Freedom in Christ is too threatening because it lies beyond their control.

The acclaim Jesus received quickly turned sour when He refused to perform for His townspeople (see Luke 4:23). When He declared an ever-widening ministry that would include all who would receive Him, anger erupted at His sermon.

The Nazareth experience typified His entire ministry. Both loved and hated, fawned upon and feared, sought out and rejected, He knew extraordinary popularity and bitter rejection (see verses 22, 28, 29).

On that Sabbath Jesus not only proclaimed the essentials of the kingdom but also explained the scope of His mission. Each one of us is the widow from Sidon or Naaman the Syrian because Christ is our Elijah and Elisha, giving help without thought of race or position (see verses 26, 27).

Jesus used the Sabbath to give healing and forgiveness, to grant troubled souls true rest. More than once Luke has the Sabbath launching a new initiative or marking a critical point in the plan of salvation (see verses 31-36). The Sabbath was not to be metered hours of conformity and formalism, but a time to rest and become new, whole, and complete in Christ.

No wonder the ordinary people find Him so wonderful, so refreshing. He leaves us astounded with the scope of His vision. His yes to the Sabbath broke it free from the prison box of legalism and made it an occasion for the celebration of wholeness.

"The teaching of Christ was the expression of an inwrought conviction and experience, and those who learn of Him become teachers after the divine order. The word of God, spoken by one who is himself sanctified through it, has a life-giving power that makes it attractive to the hearers, and convicts them that it is a living reality. . . . He makes known that which he himself has heard, seen, and handled of the word of life, that others may have fellowship with him through the knowledge of Christ." [8]

[1] Eduard Schweizer, *The Good News According to Luke,* p. 72.
[2] *The Desire of Ages,* p. 104.
[3] *Ibid.,* pp. 111, 112.
[4] Isaac Watts, "Come, Holy Spirit," *The SDA Hymnal,* No. 269.
[5] Paul S. Minear, *To Heal and to Reveal,* p. 98.
[6] Schweizer, p. 82.
[7] *The Desire of Ages,* p. 117.
[8] *Ibid.,* p. 142.

Jesus Does It All

Luke 4:38-6:49

The mighty deeds of Jesus spill over from the pages of Luke's Gospel. A cataract of miracles and teachings channels out to irrigate the dry, sin-struck lives of desperate men and women.

Driving through the rain-parched interior of Australia, you think you see a mirage of pasture and orchard wavering on the horizon. To your delight it turns from shimmering lure to reality. Water channeled, pumped, and sprayed makes the difference. To Palestine came the Water of Life, and a harvest of righteousness has appeared ever since.

For Those Who Follow Jesus: Service to Others

The objects of one of the cruel discriminations of Jesus' day received His special attention. He said yes to women. He made it clear that they too could receive the full benefit of God's saving action, with all of its power and privilege.

When Jesus ministers to us, as He did to Peter's mother-in-law, we minister in turn to Him (see Luke 4:38, 39). Service in Jesus' name springs from the way He answers our needs. He is servant to man that we might be servants to mankind. Women who minister, like the Mary who washed Jesus' feet, and Dorcas, instruct us in our responsibility to others.

The man in the synagogue had shrieked at the top of

his voice, "I know who you are—the Holy One of God" (verse 34, NEB). Again and again devils testified to Jesus, "You are the Son of God" (verse 41, NEB).

A life possessed by sin and evil cannot be a public relations officer for God. No matter how insistent the cries, the witness of evil threatens Jesus' mission. The shoutings of the demon-possessed may have confused the people about Christ's mission (see Luke 11:14). But the soul rescued from evil may be the most potent of servants.

The pressures and tensions of service sent Jesus to God in prayer (Luke 5:15, 16). When life gets hectic, go to the place of prayer. When you cannot face another person, look Him in the face. When you are at the screaming point, call out to the Prince of Peace. When burnout singes your spirit, apply the Balm of Gilead.

The great crowd that forced Him into Simon's boat (verses 1-3) showed how much Jesus needed help. But He wanted human aid only if those He called recognized His true power—power that worked in moments of frustration and defeat (as in verses 5, 6) as well as in times of abundant popularity.

Failure to give Jesus the opportunity to show His power may deny us success. If we know when and where to catch fish, then how can He help us? Peter had to submit to Jesus' will. He had to know that Jesus could far exceed the limits of his own skill and experience. Service for God knows where power resides. Not alone, but in Jesus' name and with the assistance of others (see verse 7), will success come. When we have tried it all, when we know it cannot work, when we toil wearily without success, then we, like Peter, should say, "At Your word, Master, we will let down the nets."

Setting captives free and healing the brokenhearted (Luke 4:18) brings us to the pitiful and helpless heirs of human degradation (see Luke 5:12). Lepers had to live in hovels at a distance from both dwellings and thoroughfares. They had to keep their distance from the whole and healthy.

"Israel had been called to be holy, and the Old Testament religion was based on the assumption that the way to be holy was to avoid defilement by contact with uncleanness, physical, ceremonial, or moral. Jesus believed that true holiness could not be contaminated by anything from outside (Luke 11:37-40), and that to be holy was to be like God, merciful to the afflicted (Luke 6:36). He therefore did what no Jew would do—He touched the leper, and, instead of incurring uncleanness, made the man clean."[1]

From the leper came the desperate cry for acceptance and healing (Luke 5:12). If he were clean, society would open to him. In our culture, in our churches and homes, longing hearts plead for acceptance. The spirit of apartheid permeates the human condition. Everywhere it awaits the Lord and His church, who may proclaim its victims accepted and cleansed (see verse 13).

For Those in Need: The Forgiving Son of Man

With urgency God's helpers bring the lost into the place of salvation (see verse 18). Like the servant in the parable of the great banquet, they "compel" people to come to Christ (see Luke 14:23). A motivated church will pick up the needy and bring them to the Master. They will break through the roof (see Luke 5:19) of indifference and prejudice. Members will lay the needy ones at the feet of the Healer.

To bring people into the sphere of forgiveness surpasses even physical healing. Jesus said to the paralytic, "Man, your sins are forgiven you" (verse 20, NEB). The religious leaders blinked, considered, and then silently attacked (see verse 21). How dare He assume divine power over sin! But the saving Lord and the caring church reject anything that limits the right to salvation.

When Adventist missionaries first entered Papua New Guinea, the major denominations had divided the islands into neat packages and assigned areas to one another. Even today such ideas still appear. A recent law proposed by one government minister would have carved the country up into segments for each of the churches, now including the Adventists. Jesus refused to let the leaders of His day isolate people, lock them into categories. He proclaimed liberty. So must we.

One of the great rabbis said, "A sick man does not recover from his sickness until all his sins are forgiven." Such ideas led the Pharisees to despise the sick. Jesus ministered to the whole man. To proclaim forgiveness, and for it to be effective, meant far more than physical healing, but Jesus had the authority to do both (verses 23, 24).

"Though the minds and bodies of men, their daily life and their human relationships, are all important in the eyes of Jesus, the fact remains that salvation consists primarily 'in the forgiveness of their sins' (Luke 1:77, RSV). . . . With whatever more obvious 'paralysis' I may come to Jesus, this is the real deep need which His eye perceives and to which His word of power is addressed." [2]

For the first time in Luke we meet the expression "Son of man" (Luke 5:24). Jesus used it of Himself more than 80 times in the four Gospels. For His hearers, "Son of man" surely brought Daniel's prophecy to mind (Dan. 7:13). Scribes and sectarian leaders speculated about the Son of man. Now Jesus claimed the title for Himself. What could this mean?

The Son of man carried with Him the hopes of the nation. Through Him the kingdom would come again to Israel (see Dan. 7:27). And through Him God's judgment would favor God's people (verse 22). In heaven the Son of man represented the best hopes for Israel's future (verse 14). Should the people believe Jesus, that He was the Son of man? Was the people's Representative now on earth? Would He take from the Temple service the right to declare sinners forgiven and clean? Were they now in the time of judgment? Would the kingdom go to this Galilean?

No wonder the people who witnessed the healing of the paralytic said among themselves, "You would never believe the things we have seen today" (Luke 5:26, NEB).

For the Outcasts: Joy and Acceptance

Tax gatherers fell into two main classes. Levi probably worked for a tax contractor such as Zacchaeus. He sat at the tollgate that regulated and taxed the flow of commerce into Capernaum (see verse 27). "No doubt most of the tax farmers were Jews. . . . Payment was ruthlessly exacted"[3]

Even duty collectors like Levi found ways to increase their wealth beyond an honest income. Levi left all that his former life represented and gave himself fully to the Master's service. Have we done as much?

Pharisees and scribes regarded Levi as a sinner. "The term 'sinners' means: (1) people who lead an immoral life (e.g., adulterers, swindlers, Luke 18:11) and (2) people who followed a dishonourable calling (i.e., an occupation which notoriously involved immorality or dishonesty), and who were on that account deprived of civil rights, such as holding office, or bearing witness in legal proceedings. For example, excisemen, tax collectors, shepherds, donkey drivers, pedlars, and tanners."[4]

Jesus rejected such lists. Yet, if we examine our thoughts, even we may have people preferences. Our Saviour declared all acceptable and called them to come for acceptance. Dare we do less?

Throughout His ministry the leaders charged Jesus with eating with sinners (as in Luke 5:30). Jesus' parable in verses 36-39 comments on the leaders' prejudice. The world will say, "We are OK, but what about you?" As so often happens, the very ones who think they know the answers to man's needs stand most in need themselves. Those who understand how needy they are can best receive God's help.

In Jesus' day it wasn't so much what one ate but who one did it with. Company at the table showed the kind of persons acceptable to you (see verses 31, 32). Jesus, a religious leader, startled the other religious leaders by dining with "sinners," and so declaring all potentially clean of sin.

"Celsus, the pagan critic of Christianity, complains that ordinarily those invited to participate in religious solemnities are the pure who live an honorable life. Christians, however, invite anyone who is a sinner, or foolish, or simpleminded. In short, any unfortunate will be accepted in the kingdom of God."[5]

Jesus had a supreme purpose: "Joy to the poor; for Christ had come to make them heirs of His kingdom. Joy to the rich; for He would teach them how to secure eternal riches. Joy to the ignorant; He would make them wise unto salvation."[6]

Forgiveness is stamped on the other side of the coin marked repentance. Some of the Pharisees may have opposed John's summons to repentance. Now they called him up as a better example than Jesus (see verse 33)! But Jesus declared that a world given the joy of forgiveness ought to expect joyful practices as long as the Son remained with them (verse 34). A time for mourning would come, but not yet!

Can we accept the joy of being forgiven and of forgiving others? Do the old skins of tradition and prejudice restrict the power of Christ in our lives? The world needs new skins—changed lives—to contain the marvelous power of Christ and pour it out to the needy world (see verses 36-39).

Luke, the theologian, proclaims God's new order, one differing sharply from that insisted upon by the religious leaders. Jesus creates the new age. His names and His deeds declare Him divine. Luke links Him back to the Old Testament prophecies and to the covenant promises. In Christ we perceive their true purposes as Jesus continues God's saving actions.

For His Disciples: New Authority

Commencing in Luke 5:30, the lifestyle of Jesus and the disciples comes under attack. In Luke 6 Jesus rejects severe and unauthorized Sabbath restrictions. "His authority for acting in such a way is that He is the Son of man (Luke 6:5) who sits (Luke 22:69) or stands (Acts 7:56) at the right hand of God. He is also an interpreter of the law whose stance is validated by the healing miracle in Luke 6:9, 10. Anyone who does not listen to Him will be cut off from the people (Acts 3:22, 23). Overall, the section Luke 5:30-6:11 shows Jesus as a 'sign that is spoken against' (Luke 2:34, RSV)."[7]

At first glance His disciples appear to have blundered badly. Taking grain from the field on a Sabbath offended the strict Pharisees (Luke 6:1, 2). But Jesus defended the joy of the freedom of true Sabbathkeeping. He is Lord of the Sabbath, and therefore of the law and of creation itself. Far from diminishing the significance of the Sabbath, Jesus enhanceed it (verse 5). He invites us to concentrate on the garden of beauty that is the Sabbath rather than on the security system His compatriots had erected to preserve it (see verses 9, 10).

For His People: The Law of Love

Luke 6:12 begins an episode in Christ's life that has parallels with the giving of the law to Moses. Like Moses, Jesus went up a mountain to commune with God. He singled out from His disciples those who would "rule" His church (see verses 13-15). Returning from the mountain, He proclaimed the new law to His disciples, the new Israel of God.

Three groups of people heard the sermon that followed: the apostles (the twelve), the disciples, and the crowd who had not yet decided about Jesus. Matthew places the sermon on a mountainside (Matt. 5:1, 2). Luke seems to place the location on a plain (see Luke 6:17). While geography has importance, remember that one can regard the same piece of land in different ways, depending on the individual's perspective.

Our Saviour is also our teacher, the giver of the law of love, which must now govern our actions. What it means to live in the kingdom of God He clearly defines. "The followers of Jesus, like the godly people described in the Psalms and wisdom literature, are literally poor and downtrodden, whereas many of those who reject the gospel enjoy material plenty. Riches can keep men out of the kingdom of God, and disciples must be prepared for poverty by worldly standards."[8]

The One who will separate the sheep from the goats at the last day even now is discerning what the judgment will confirm (see verse 23). Those who are in need, those who hunger, will feast at the Messianic banquet. Mourning will turn to joy (Isa. 60:20; 61:3; Jer. 31:13). God will secure their faith despite persecution and misrepresentation.

In Christ our love extends to the unlovely and the unlovable. "Jesus did not tell His disciples to fall in love with their enemies or to feel for them as they felt for their families and friends. *Agape* is a gracious, determined, and active interest in the true welfare of others, which is not deterred even by hatred, cursing, and abuse, not limited by calculation of deserts or results, based solely on the nature of God."[9]

For the Christian to revenge, to retaliate, to pay back,

even against uncalled-for aggression, surrenders the life to evil (see Luke 6: 28-30). Before, evil controlled only one person; now it possesses two. Most people have an idea of what is fair or just. That is not enough. Jesus calls us to the good and the holy.

All too often we seek our own happiness and ask others to be virtuous. Love invites us to be virtuous, and our neighbors will be happier. The law of love directs us to the welfare of others.

In Christ's cause His followers give and give and give again (see verse 30). Not that He is looking for unworldly paupers! But the Christian should not hold back for love of material possessions. Love will give everything if need be.

Jesus said, "Be ye . . . merciful, as your Father also is merciful" (verse 36). In Matthew Jesus urged, "Be ye . . . perfect" (Matt. 5:48). Is our Lord asking less in Luke than in Matthew? Hardly. There is a perfecting of love that will know no favorites, neither enemy nor friend. When we have heard the yes of God's mercy, the demand is on us to extend a yes of mercy, love, and forgiveness to all.

Hillel, the great Jewish rabbi, said, "What is hateful to thee, do not to another. That is the whole law and all else is explanation." Philo of Alexandria, the first-century Jewish philosopher, commented, "What you hate to suffer, do not do to anyone else." Confucius urged, "What you do not want done to yourself, do not do to others."

"Every one of these forms is negative. It is not unduly difficult to keep yourself from such action; but it is a very difficult thing to go out of your way to do to others what you would want them to do to you. The very essence of Christian conduct is that it consists, not in refraining from bad things, but in actively doing good things." [10]

The true comparison isn't between what we were and what we now are, nor is it with one another. The true comparison is between us and God. How needy we are!

And who but He the source of help?

"According to the light we possess we must distinguish between good and evil and in His power first combat the evil in ourselves and then in others. But we are never to encroach upon God's right to judge and to condemn. We must avoid all censoriousness and revengefulness, and forgive those who have sinned against us."[11]

Where the searcher for guidance goes for instruction makes all the difference (see Luke 6:39, 40). The level you will reach in spiritual understanding, in mercy and compassion, may depend on the teacher from whom you learn.

The search for truth does not always look for proofs. Jesus came with truth and asked for belief, for our trust. In believing Him we will find truth (see verses 46, 47).

In the parable of the fruit trees a wild or untended tree will produce sour, bitter, or useless fruit (verses 43, 44). (If you do not know the difference between a kumquat and a California navel orange, just taste them!) A good man will bear good action (verse 45). Those who hear Jesus will not simply chant, "Lord, Lord," like a sort of mantra. They will do what He commands.

As Jesus brought the sermon to a close He drove home the point of action rather than just mental consent. Building on the rock represents hearing and then doing (verses 47, 48); building the house without foundations, hearing but not doing (verse 49). Crises will test us. Events may put our character under severe stress. The final judgment will try all men. A rocklike life of obedience provides stability and security. No life will collapse with Christ as its firm foundation.

> My hope is built on nothing less
> Than Jesus' blood and righteousness;

> I dare not trust the sweetest frame,
> But wholly lean on Jesus' name.
> On Christ, the solid Rock, I stand;
> All other ground is sinking sand,
> All other ground is sinking sand.[12]

"He longs to see His children reveal a character after His similitude. As the sunbeam imparts to the flowers their varied and delicate tints, so does God impart to the soul the beauty of His own character."[13]

---

[1] G. B. Caird, *Saint Luke*, p. 92.

[2] Michael Wilcock, *The Savior of the World*, p. 70.

[3] Joachim Jeremias, *Jerusalem in the Time of Jesus*, p. 32.

[4] _____, *The Parables of Jesus*, p. 132.

[5] Charles H. Talbert, *Reading Luke*, p. 64.

[6] *The Desire of Ages*, p. 277.

[7] Talbert, pp. 65, 66.

[8] I. Howard Marshall, *The Gospel of Luke*, p. 246.

[9] Caird, p. 104.

[10] William Barclay, trans., *The Gospel of Luke*, The Daily Study Bible Series, p. 79.

[11] Norval Geldenhuys, *Commentary on the Gospel of Luke*, p. 213.

[12] Edward Mote, "My Hope Is Built on Nothing Less," *The SDA Hymnal*, No. 522.

[13] *The Desire of Ages*, p. 313.

The Kingdom Overflows in Blessing

Luke 7:1-9:50

We had sung, "God be with you till we meet again." Now they came, saying farewell. For a week my wife and I had shared the blessings of a Week of Prayer with them.

Each brought us a gift, a shell lei to circle the neck. Thank you, the lei said, you will surely return. When weighed at the airport, the leis pushed the scales to 84 pounds! Ah! the overwhelming affection and generosity! The love of our church members poured itself out and flowed around us, blessing and sustaining.

The Gospel writers, and with Luke at the fore, show how Jesus fulfilled Ephesians 2:6, 7. "And in union with Christ Jesus he [God] raised us up and enthroned us with him in the heavenly realms, so that he might display in the ages to come how immense are the resources of his grace, and how great his kindness to us in Christ Jesus" (NEB).

Jesus lifted the fallen and downtrodden and gave them a place in His kingdom. He showed the kindness of God, the compassion of Heaven, toward the weakest. In story form we read the most profound insights into the grace of God.

To the Unlikely and the Unworthy

The concern of the centurion for his servant (Luke 7:2, 3) contrasted with the callous attitude of the Pharisees when Jesus healed the man with the withered arm (Luke

6:7-9). (Later Jesus would remark on the compassion of a Samaritan toward one of another race [Luke 10:33-35].) The Roman officer valued his servant for himself, not just because of his skills or the service.

A person with rocklike faith never doubts God and His power. Jesus found such a person in this Roman. The man's character revealed where he was building his life (see Luke 6:47, 48). His concern for his servant showed that the fruit of the kingdom could grow where others least expected it (see verses 43-45).

The Jewish leaders hated the Roman rulers of their land. The Zealots pledged themselves to throw out the conquerors or die in the attempt. Yet this kindly foreigner, a despised Gentile, had won the affection of the Jewish community leaders (Luke 7:4, 5).

Consider the characteristics of his faith:

1. It showed no presumption, but trusted its case to Jesus (verse 7).

2. It came in humility. "I am not worthy that thou shouldest enter under my roof" (verse 6).

3. It accepted Jesus' power without question (verses 7, 8).

The elders commended the centurion for his good works (verses 4, 5), but Jesus healed the servant because of his faith (see verse 9).

In the world of Jewish expectations, the Messiah would, like Elijah, bring life to the dead. But could it ever really happen again? Were such events forever lost in the past?

We share the same hope of resurrection. Do you have an only son, as did the widow of Nain, who is gone? Do you long to see loved ones again? The story of Luke 7:11-16 holds hope for all who trust in Christ.

Fly, lingering moments, fly, O, fly,

> Dear Savior, quickly come!
> We long to see Thee as Thou art,
> And reach that blissful home.[1]

"His heart went out" to the mother (verse 13, NEB). The funeral procession offended Him. Why should death always conquer? Should not the Giver of life wipe away tears (Rev. 21:4)? That day Death trembled because of the final rout waiting in its future (see Rev. 20:14). That day God said yes to life for all who have faith in the Life-Giver (see Luke 7:14).

To the Wise Who Trust

From the crowds that followed Jesus, a number of the disciples of John watched the miracles, including the raising of the widow's son (see verse 18). What did they tell the Baptist? How could he have doubted that Jesus was the hoped-for Messiah? Perhaps, because Herod's bars blocked off his faith. Circumstances draw blinds across the vision of faith (see verse 20). Hopes fade. Doubts grow. Despair tortures.

Doubt, not despair, is the opposite of hope. Hope peoples the future with positive possibilities; doubt, with negative ones. Jesus sought the defeat of doubt through the hope He brought.

Did the Baptist look for a fiery judgment on the land (Luke 3:7), as did Jonah at Nineveh? Did John anticipate a sudden end of sin as the Lamb of God brought grace and forgiveness to Israel? Unfortunately, wrong expectations destroy trust. "Happy is the man who does not find me a stumbling-block" (Luke 7:23, NEB). Trust lets God create hope.

"Wisdom," Jesus said, "is justified of all her children" (verse 35). The children who would play neither weddings nor funerals missed out on any game (see verse 32).

In the ancient East, weddings and funerals passed through the streets frequently with much display, loud music, and dancing. Children loved the noise and color.

The wise remain open to God whenever He speaks. The people showed wisdom (verse 29), while the "wise" leaders proved foolish (verse 30). The plan of God had its justification as the people responded to God's prophets.

Most probably on the Sabbath, Jesus accepted an invitation to eat at Simon's house (verse 36). He invited the Master home as a church elder might ask the preacher home today. Custom permitted those attending the service—and other interested persons—to follow the luncheon party home and stand around in the open courtyard, observing the meal and listening to the conversation. Mary came with the curious and the interested. However, her purpose differed from idle curiosity. She came overflowing with love for the Master (see verses 37, 38).

The very idea of a prostitute entering a Pharisee's house and accosting one of the guests boggles the mind. Only through her new sense of self-worth that Jesus had given her could she have ever done so. Jesus said yes to her. In Him she was free to be herself and pour out her love in service to Christ.

The Great Physician gave self-esteem to those whom He saved. They discovered their worth in His love for them. Only as we know our true value in Christ can we value others enough to care for them and love them, however they may regard us.

As the tears fell Mary saw the water marks on the dusty feet of Jesus. Forgetful of where she was, she unbound her hair, something no woman would do in public, and used it as a towel. She opened the expensive vial of perfume, hung from a cord around her neck, and massaged it into His tired feet. The heart that knows Jesus' love holds back nothing.

When Jesus finally turned to Simon He did not rail at him, but spoke in kindly reproof. Had Simon, a Pharisee, been so afraid of ritual pollution that he would not touch, let alone kiss, Jesus, a known friend of sinners (see verses 44, 45)? Did he so begrudge a kindness to the Lord that he would not even send to the kitchen for olive (cooking) oil (verse 46)?

Mary showed how love must work. When Christ takes over, nothing is too good, no service too great, no sacrifice too big, for Him.

Yet not love but faith saves. Roman Catholic theologians use this story to attempt to prove that penance and good works performed in love bring acceptance from God. But neither the Greek original nor the English translation permits this interpretation. Lest doubt should rise, Jesus made it plain: "Thy faith hath saved thee; go in peace" (verse 50).

Eastern women took no part in public life. When a Jewess left her house she hid her face behind two veils, making recognition impossible. Custom forbade a man to be alone with a woman or to greet her in the street. "The daughters of the leading houses in Jerusalem, who were strict in the observance of the Law, were accustomed to stay within the house before marriage, as far as possible; married women left it only with their faces covered."[2]

But there were exceptions. On the Day of Atonement young women danced before the young men in the vineyards around Jerusalem. A wife helped her husband sell their wares. Maidens went to the well for water, and married women worked in the fields.

A man acquired a wife. In marriage the exchange of money, the signing of a legal contract, followed the same principles as for a slave. Unlike a slave, she could hold property, but could not dispose of it without her husband's consent. If the husband died or he divorced her, the marriage contract dictated what would be paid to the bride's family. Polygamy occurred, the concubine having no marriage contract and being even more at risk socially.

Males dominated religious life. Girls did not go to school. According to a conservative scribe (Rabbi Eliezer, A.D. 90), to teach a daughter the Torah was like teaching her lechery. The first part of the synagogue service was open to women, but the section given to the teaching of the scribes was for men. Only rarely did women place their hands on the sacrificial victim at the Temple or take part in the wave offering.

"It is typical that joy reigned at the birth of a boy, while the birth of a daughter was often greeted with indifference, even with sorrow. We have therefore the impression that Judaism in Jesus' time also had a very low opinion of women, which is usual in the Orient where she is chiefly valued for her fecundity, kept as far as possible shut away from the outer world, submissive to the power of her father or her husband, and where she is inferior to men from a religious point of view." [3]

Yet Jesus drew the circle of divine love around women. They came to the kingdom on precisely the same basis as men (see Luke 8:1-3).

Luke began his Gospel with Zecharias, but Mary quickly assumed heroine status (Luke 1:5; verse 28). Anna joined Simeon as witness to the coming of the Messiah (Luke 2:25, 26; verses 36, 38). A mother had her son raised, and a father his daughter (Luke 7:12-15; 8:41, 42, 49-55). The story of the insistent man paralleled the story of the insistent woman (Luke 11:5-8; 18:1-8). First the story of the lawyer, and then the story of two good women (Luke 10:25-37; verses 38-42). A woman healed on the Sabbath, and then a man (Luke 13:10-17; 14:1-6). Both a daughter of Abraham and a son of Abraham received the Saviour's blessing (Luke 13:13, 16; 19:9). A shepherd, and a woman, searched for the lost (Luke 15:3-7; verses 8-10). A man sowed mustard seed, and a woman leavened a loaf (Luke 13:19; verse 21), and two men and two women were separated at the coming of Jesus (see Luke 17:34, 35). Luke presented men and women on a much more equal plane than was common at the time.

In the Good News

God sows the world with His word (see Luke 8:11). His Spirit scatters the seeds of the kingdom abroad, and the harvest will surely come (verses 5-8).

The parable of the sower related to Jesus' work for the people. Vast crowds flocked to listen. Some accepted, others scoffed.

In Palestine at that time, plowing occurred *after* sowing. The seed remained exposed or was planted in thin soil on the rocky places. Beaten tracks also resisted the plow, so the seed that fell there didn't get covered. Grain that fell in such places died from lack of moisture or from being trodden to death, or was eaten by birds.

Here Jesus does not grade success: all good seed yields a hundredfold (cf. Matt. 13:8; Mark 4:8). The thousands baptized in Mexico and the tens in Europe are all "an hundredfold." To act on the Word is to produce the right harvest (see Luke 8:20, 21). God has set the light of truth before all men so that nothing remains hidden (verses 16, 17).

The life governed by the Word grows and produces fruit. But in the life not governed by the Word, Satan, the slanderer, steals the seed from the life, confuses the mind, and sends temptation (see verses 11, 12).

Jesus reflected on those who believed for a while and then gave up (verses 13, 14), something all too frequent in Christian communities. Materialism and anxiety, among many other problems, stifle faith. But the good and honest heart will hold fast the Word with patience and thus bear fruit.

"Parables both reveal and conceal truth; they reveal it to the genuine seeker who will take the trouble to dig beneath the surface and discover the meaning, but they conceal it from him who is content simply to listen to the story. This is plainly the result of the parables, but Jesus says it also is their purpose. Parables are a mine of information to those who are in earnest, but they are a judgment on the casual and careless."[4]

Through His Mighty Power

Our evaluation of Jesus' power affects our ability to witness. To call Him omnipotent and then rely on ourselves, our systems, or our institutions mocks the Mighty One of Israel. Luke presents a series of stories to illustrate the power and authority of Jesus:

1. Jesus can control the elements (Luke 8:22-25).
2. Jesus has subjugated the demons (verses 26-39).
3. Jesus knows our thoughts (see verse 46).
4. Jesus has conquered death (verses 49-56).

Man lost dominion over nature. Now we live in terror of it. Disordered by sin, elemental forces demand a savage toll of life and property each year. But the disorder of Satan's domain yields at Christ's command and gives a foretaste of the order in the new creation (see verses 24, 25). "Who then is this?" (verse 25, RSV). The Man to whom God is entrusting the power and authority of His kingdom.

The chaos of a life ruled by evil also must yield to Christ's command (verse 29). The despair of the sin-tormented parallels the despair at nature out of control.

Satan knew who faced him. Demons and evil spirits acknowledged Jesus both in the Gospel and in Acts. In irony the demon tormented asked Jesus not to torture him (Luke 8:28)! How often a tormented conscience seeks to avoid the very One who can give release.

At the heart of the kingdom that Satan had once

offered Jesus (Luke 4:5, 6), Jesus now showed His power. Remember that even now Satan is defeated. God will banish him to the abyss (Rev. 20:3). Even now his cohorts are subject to such judgment (see Luke 8:31, NEB).

How can we explain the reaction of the Gadarene people to this miracle? "In the grip of a great fear" (verse 37, NEB), they put up the notice "Do Not Disturb." They wanted to be left alone without the decisions that the miracle demanded of them. Although they feared what else might happen to them besides the loss of the swine, a serious enough matter, the changes that believing in Jesus would bring terrified them even more.

Lord, keep us from the Gadarene syndrome.

Eusebius, the church historian of the early fourth century, recorded that the woman healed of her hemorrhage (verses 43-48) erected a statue in honor of Jesus. It remained until the emperor Julian had it destroyed in his attempt to restore pagan gods. He erected a statue of himself in its place, only to see it in turn destroyed by a thunderbolt.

The tragedy of the unaccepted and the unacceptable haunts Luke's picture of Palestine. The woman's bleeding made her always ceremonially unclean (Lev. 15:19-31). Her husband would despise her. Normal marriage relations would be forbidden. Nor could she participate in religious events. In touching Jesus she made Him ceremonially unclean. But He acknowledged no such barrier. Jesus welcomes our touch. He accepts us, and in Him we find worth. Even though we may never speak it, He knows our need .

Jesus told Jairus that if he would only show faith, his daughter would be well (Luke 8:50). The child would soon come of age (12½ years). Jairus' concern for her would not have been matched by many. The somewhat heartless attitude (verse 49) of the man from his household reflected the common feeling about girls.

As in the case of Lazarus, Jesus defined the nature of death. "She is asleep," He said (verse 52, NEB). To know that loved ones sleep in Jesus comforts us and turns aside the despair of death.

Natural disasters, sickness, and death march through the pages of Luke. Suffering also occurs around us, sometimes at a distance, sometimes all too near. These stories of Luke teach us the power of Jesus to go beyond human misery. The Lord does not give a solution to all tragedy, but He does offer us the power to cope (Rom. 8:37).

Through the Witness of His Followers

Jesus did not wait until after His resurrection to commission the apostles. By this point (Luke 9:1) they had seen enough to know what God could do. Now Jesus sent them out to do what He had done, declaring the good news and healing the sick. And they succeeded (verse 6)!

In the Gospels the twelve oscillated between strong faith and queasy weakness. In this passage they showed true faith.

True faith ventures out with only the power and authority God has given. It needs no stick to defend itself, no suitcase to provide comfort, temporal food taken along to nourish, or money to buy (verse 3). Such faith does not falter behind prison walls, and is willing to sleep on rough ground to do God's bidding. Satisfied with "bread and water," it keeps on when funds run out.

When I arrived in England in 1975 to take up my work there, the first item of business dealt with a cable from Africa reporting that the Nigerian government had taken over our hospital at Ile-Ife. A few years before, they had assumed control of our high schools. One learns quickly that the gospel goes on and succeeds both with and without such establishments. Not that they lack importance, but the truly important thing for the Christian is the gospel message.

Luke creates a theological sandwich for us. As the filling he tells the story of the loaves and fishes (verses 13-16). On either side he places the question "Who is this?"—once asked by Herod (verse 9), the other time as a query directed to the disciples (verse 20).

Confusion about Jesus had reigned since His birth. Even today people still want to downgrade Him—a great teacher, they might say. Others want to categorize Him—better than Buddha or Confucius. Still others reject Him—never lived, they conclude. And so on. Herod did not know, perhaps could not then know, who He was, but the disciples knew (verse 20).

Jesus asks the church to accept responsibility for the success of His work (see verse 13). We have no right to abort the progress of His mission (see verse 12). The Saviour will multiply the "loaves and . . . fishes" to meet the need of the success He has created (verse 16).

"The lesson [of the leftover food] was twofold. Nothing is to be wasted. We are to let slip no temporal advantage. We should neglect nothing that would serve to benefit a human being. . . . With the same carefulness are we to treasure the bread from heaven to satisfy the needs of the soul. By every word of God we are to live. Nothing that God has spoken is to be lost. Not one word that concerns our eternal salvation are we to neglect."[5]

Right now, as I write this, the South Pacific Division is experiencing a marvelous growth in membership in Papua New Guinea. But the question of how to feed this multitude spiritually urges itself upon us. In a subsistence culture, tithes never meet the demands of maintaining a church system. Yet the church hears the command "Give ye them to eat" (verse 13). In remarkable ways God multiplies our humble provisions.

God gives His people the means to solve the problem themselves (see verse 16). If church leaders feel that they have to answer every need personally, or that the only resources are the ones they themselves perceive, the work will never finish. Instead the Lord multiplies all resources so that the people can be fed. And with enough left over to start on the needs of the next 5,000!

But Is Not Always Understood

After a confidential discussion about who Jesus is (verses 18-22), Jesus told the disciples, The Son of man will suffer (verse 22). So too will all who seek the way of Christ (verse 23). True faith and obedience will lead to persecution, sacrifice, slander, perhaps even death. But do not confuse such things with the common lot of man, with its disappointments, disease, injustice, and hardship.

Jesus calls us to take up the cross (verse 23), to be willing to die in shame and agony. The world mocks faith and crucifies the faithful. As we cling to the cross, it turns the world against us, and we "die daily" (1 Cor. 15:31).

The Son of man, who acts always in favor of God's people, will find no reason to acknowledge any who distance themselves from Him (Luke 9:26). He will not give them the kingdom (see Dan. 7:27).

The kingdom of God operates around us continually (see Luke 9:27). We are of the generation that knows its power. *This generation* has a wide application and is not restricted in time if properly applied:

1. Jesus had spoken of martyrdom (verse 22). Some of those who would be martyred (to "taste death" [verse 27] meant to die as a martyr) would see the kingdom of God. They saw the kingdom of God in the growth of the church.

2. He spoke unto all (verse 23). He emphasized the fate of those who reject Him (verses 24-26). All includes this present age, which likewise has decisions to make about Jesus.

3. Some will not taste death (that is, go through the

bitter experience of martyrdom) until they have seen evidence of the kingdom of God (verse 27). Pentecost came before the first martyr died.

4. The kingdom of God is not a separate event from what was then occurring. What the disciples lived carried with it the character of the kingdom (verses 23, 24). In what was happening and in the events of the Resurrection, the Ascension, Pentecost, and the Second Coming, they were seeing and would "see the kingdom of God."

Luke drops into an Old Testament, biblical style of language during his telling of the Transfiguration story and the following event. In this way he conveys the mystery of the Transfiguration. Note the three-time use of "and it came to pass" (verses 28, 33, 37), and the double use of "and, behold" (verses 30, 38), followed by "and, lo" (verse 39).

God said, "This is my beloved Son: hear him" (verse 35). The Lord proclaimed His yes to the Son so that the whole cosmos might hear. Yet Herod could ask about Jesus (verse 9) but never really experience who He is. Thus it is with the majority. Peter, like the minority, confessed Jesus (verse 20), and heard the voice of God declare His identity (verse 35). It is not who you are that brings God's revelation, but whether you hear Him, His beloved Son.

Even when God makes things so plain, we can still stumble in perplexity and incomprehension. It is not that God keeps things secret, but rather that we are so dull.

Luke used two incidents to point up this incomprehension. First, to insert human values into divine plans shows up our stupidity (verse 46). Of what point will greatness in the kingdom be, seeing that all will gather in awe around the Lamb? To claim to know better than God where He would lead (verse 49), only makes fools of those who call themselves disciples.

"Immaturity also is a recurrent blight on the life of the church. Not that I am out for personal glory, of course—but I do think people ought to recognize my *status*, since I am after all the Reverend (or Doctor, or sir, or whatever). . . . Or, more subtly, I may be tempted to what one might call pride of *affiliation*, when I stick up not for myself but for my group or organization. In each case, though, there is a lack of the humility which enables the Christian to look 'not only to his own interests, but also to the interests of others' (Phil. 2:4, RSV); and it is a lack which bedevils again and again the growth of unity among the people of God."[6]

> O God of light, Your Word, a lamp unfailing,
> Shall pierce the darkness of our earthbound way
> And show Your grace, Your plan for us unveiling,
> And guide our footsteps to the perfect day.[7]

[1] "How Cheering Is the Christian's Hope," *The SDA Hymnal*, No. 440.

[2] Joachim Jeremias, *Jerusalem in the Time of Jesus*, p. 361.

[3] *Ibid.*, p. 375.

[4] Leon Morris, *Luke: An Introduction and Commentary*, p. 152.

[5] *The Ministry of Healing*, p. 48.

[6] Michael Wilcock, *The Savior of the World*, pp. 112, 113.

[7] Sarah E. Taylor, "O God of Light," *The SDA Hymnal*, No. 275.

God Gives
Much More

Luke 9:51-11:54

Did you ever feel that God asks too much of you?

Simeon Stylites perched himself atop a column for more than three decades, thinking God had asked it of him. In Mexico City I watched as a man on his knees inched his way across a huge cobblestone square. If he might arrive this way inside the Shrine of Guadalupe, then perhaps, he thought, God would notice and honor him.

The Gospels present a different view of God. We ask. He gives. Jesus said, "How much more shall your heavenly Father give . . . to them that ask?" (Luke 11:13).

The Gospel of Luke takes a decided turn at chapter 9:51: "As the time approached when he was to be taken up to heaven, he set his face resolutely towards Jerusalem" (NEB). Ancient literature often employed the format of travel to feature the words and actions of its heroes. Homer's *Odyssey* and Virgil's *Aeneid* both use a journey as a structure for telling their story. Luke followed a similar model in both his Gospel and Acts.

Though we know from the other Gospels that Jesus visited Jerusalem on a number of occasions during His ministry, Luke portrays just one visit. Jerusalem held suffering, death, and glory for Jesus. In that city the prophecies would find fulfillment. The Son of man would die and be resurrected, and the Spirit would fall. To come to Jerusalem was to come to crisis.

Jesus, God's Giver

The journey had hardly begun when a brush with the Samaritans flared up (Luke 9:52, 53). Relations between the two nations had fluctuated through the years. Hatred had caused many violent incidents. Galilean Jews, headed for Jerusalem by the shortest route, had to pass through Samaritan territory. Josephus relates that in A.D. 52 they ambushed and killed Galilean pilgrims. In revenge a Jewish war party swept in and attacked Samaritan villages.

What if God gives life to someone you hate or despise? Can you say yes to that? (See verses 55, 56.)

James and John thought the Samaritans expendable (verse 54). About 150 years before, John Hyrcanus had captured Shechem and destroyed the Samaritan temple. Less than 20 years before Jesus began His ministry, the Samaritans invaded the Jewish Temple and strewed human bones even in the Most Holy Place. To the mind of a Jew, fire from heaven would not be too much in revenge for such an appalling sacrilege!

When the Pharisees had criticized Jesus for eating and drinking with sinners, He had said, "I came not to call the righteous, but sinners to repentance" (Luke 5:32). And when at a later time the crowd at Jericho murmured about Jesus eating with Zacchaeus, He spoke of having come "to seek and to save that which was lost" (Luke 19:10). Now, in response to the fierce thoughts of the sons of Zebedee, He replied, "The Son of man is not come to destroy men's lives, but to save them" (Luke 9:56).

Jesus taught tolerance. Christians would need it in the future. His apostles must learn to grant religious liberty to others even though those others did not give it to them.

A demand for comfort and security found no echo in Jesus' lifestyle. Hear the piteous words "The Son of man hath not where to lay his head" (verse 58). He "made himself of no reputation" (Phil. 2:7), taking on Himself a servant's role. Jesus never booked ahead at the next Holiday Inn. He carried no checkbook or credit card.

Heaven's priorities are crystal clear. What about ours? Proper burial was most important to Jews (see Luke 9:59), but this must be left to others. What a risk we run when we put worldly things first, thinking that if we hurry, we can catch up with Jesus later (see verse 60)!

Not even time to say goodbye? No, said Jesus. I am on My way. Do not let anything slow down your response to My call (see verse 62). Earlier in Galilee He had attended a farewell party given by Levi-Matthew (see Luke 5:29). But with the approaching crisis, His priorities changed.

Our mission begins in Jesus (see Luke 10:1) and gives Him the glory (verse 17). We have no detail of where the seventy went. Instead, the mission focuses on Jesus, the author and goal of all Christian endeavor.

Luke alone recorded the double sending, first of the apostles, then of the seventy. "Luke's reason for this 'doublet' seems to be that the 'mission' will not be restricted to the twelve; 'others' will share in the testimony to be borne to Jesus and His own word or message. The significance of this 'doublet' is realized when one recalls how in Acts the role of the twelve eventually becomes insignificant."[1]

God owns the harvest (verse 2). The reaping is gathering souls into the kingdom. Success in harvesting depends on Jesus and on prayer (verse 2). How often Luke exalts intercessory prayer!

Here we have a model for our methods as we go on Christ's errand. Go two by two (verse 1). Pray for others to share the task (verse 2). Enter as innocents into the fierce and hostile world of unrepentant sin (verse 3). Carry peace from the Lord (verse 5).

One decision ("the son of peace" [verse 6]) may expand enormously. One individual opens the way for whole families, clans, and even tribes to hear the message.

"The important thing, therefore, is not triumphant missionary success but the chance to open others to *this* road, which often enough foregoes visible victories. In addition there is the sending 'two by two' (RSV), as a corrective to all self-aggrandizement and fixation on favorite notions, and the renunciation of all forms of security, trust in advertizing, management, rhetoric, and mass enthusiasm. . . . A church that ceases to take seriously the fact of unbelief, whatever its basis, can itself no longer be taken seriously in its proclamation of belief and faith." [2]

> Send them forth with morn's first beaming,
> Send them in the noontide's glare;
> When the sun's last rays are streaming,
> Bid them gather everywhere.
> Lord of harvest, send forth reapers!
> Hear us, Lord, to Thee we cry;
> Send them now the sheaves to gather,
> Ere the harvesttime pass by. [3]

Jesus pointed to the judgment (verse 14). Through His messengers He visits the towns and cities of this earth. Those who reject His envoys will suffer a worse fate than Sodom (see verse 12). Some would "see the kingdom of God" before tasting death (Luke 9:27). Through the act of preaching, the "kingdom of God is come nigh" (Luke 10:9, 11) to each person who hears. Judgment is based on the opportunity to learn as well as on what the individual does actually know. Thus the people of Bethsaida had been evangelized and had witnessed the feeding of the 5,000 (Luke 9:10-17). Capernaum had had many miracles performed in its streets (see Luke 4:23). The inhabitants of the two villages would be judged by their response to His activities in them.

Luke, writing some 30 years after the events of the gospel, had specific communities of Christians in mind. It fascinates us to see how like us they were. For example, the news section of the *Adventist Review* attracts us because there we find the record of the wonders of the gospel's progress. How we rejoice at the success of the message.

It's right to say, "In Your name, Lord, this or that happened" (see verse 17). Remember, any victory that we gain rests on His victory. He has defeated Satan (see verse 18), therefore we may succeed. Even the serpents of doubt and the scorpions of despair die before the one who trusts in the Lord (verse 19).

Sir James Simpson introduced the use of chloroform as an anesthetic. When asked what he felt was his most important discovery, he did not reply, "Chloroform," but said, "My greatest discovery was that Jesus Christ is my Saviour." Our joy lies in His salvation, in having our names written in heaven.

"Satan in his efforts to deceive and tempt our race had thought to frustrate the divine plan in man's creation; but Christ now asks that this plan be carried into effect as if man had never fallen. He asks for His people not only pardon and justification, full and complete, but a share in His glory and a seat upon His throne." [4]

More than once Luke reminds us of the joy that divine beings experience. In Luke 15:7, 10 the angels of heaven rejoice. Now in chapter 10:21 Jesus exults with joy. Why? Because God is a giver. He owns all. Therefore He gives, and gives again.

Luke here reports a threefold experience of joy. First, the joy of the seventy as they returned victorious (verse 17). Second, that of the Lord as He saw how God's power worked through His disciples (verse 21). Third, the joy of fulfillment as what the ancient prophets and kings wished for was now coming true (verses 23, 24).

But what is it that makes happy "eyes" (verse 23)? Not the deeds, but the Man. To have seen Jesus, that is the consummate joy! Some 30 years before, Simeon had rejoiced that his eyes had seen "the deliverance which thou hast made ready in full view of all the nations" (Luke 2:31, NEB).

To Give Yourself Is Godlike

Four questions outline the parable of the good Samaritan:

1. "What shall I do to inherit eternal life?" (Luke 10:25).

2. "What is written in the law? how readest thou?" (verse 26).

3. "Who is my neighbour?" (verse 29).

4. "Which now of these three . . . was neighbour unto him that fell among the thieves?" (verse 36).

New Testament Judaism had no doubt about eternal life for the *nation.* That, the Jews believed, was written in the prophets and could never be withdrawn. But what of the *individual?* What could he do to ensure himself of a place in the community that would share eternal life? Where was that very good deed or deeds that he could do that would be to his credit like a bank account? After he had deposited those good deeds, whatever he did that might displease would be offset by good. His store of good works would see him through. Did you ever feel such thoughts intrude into your religious experience?

Jesus turned the lawyer's first question back on him (verse 26). But the man squirmed away from his responsibilities. "Who is my neighbour?" is not a Christian question. It emerges out of a world of thinking in which one can carve up the human population into neat categories. Some you look upon as acceptable; most you reject. Which group or groups, the man asked, do you think should qualify for my charity and friendship? With whom should I dine? Whom should I avoid?

The lawyer had declared himself in favor of the commandment "Thou shalt love . . . thy neighbour as thyself" (verse 27). Now he must meet it in practical application.

Prospects of ritual uncleanness frightened the best intentioned Pharisee from contact with sick or dying people. All it needed was pus, blood, or excreta, and uncleanness followed.

Most probably the priest was returning from his stint of duty at the Temple—an opportunity given once in a lifetime. Back home in Jericho, family and his native villagers waited ready to receive him with love, gifts, and accumulated tithes and offerings. Prudence overcame any compassion he might have had, and he moved on (verse 31). And the same for the Levite (verse 32). God asks us to risk ourselves for others; to risk comfort and conformity for others' welfare.

At this time Jews thought Samaritans no better than Gentiles, considering them impure even from the cradle. Scribes declared them idolatrous because they regarded Mount Gerizim as holy. Jews could not eat food prepared by a Samaritan because of their "idolatry." The Samaritan in Christ's parable—whom the Jews regarded as God-forsaken—showed Godlike qualities, while the priest and the Levite, who thought God on their side, were truly godless.

The parable attacks all human systems and decisions that refuse pity on the needy. Jesus condemned the separatist mania in the Palestinian Judaism of His time. How can God be expected to side with such an attitude? When the love of God finally said yes to the sacrifice of His beloved Son, He showed what price that yes demanded to save us—the needy.

God sent Jesus, the great and good Samaritan, to bind up the wounded and give life to the dying. The parable recounts God's effective action for mankind when earthly systems fail. It displays the extravagance of a love that denies nothing for the one in need. Sin has wounded all. The poison of death has only one Antidote, Jesus, the Great Physician.

Three times in his Gospel Luke deplored the busyness that cuts itself off from God's action. In the parable of the sower, some bear no fruit because of the "cares . . . of this life" (Luke 8:14). In the last days God's people must watch that the cares of this life do not lead them into a trap (Luke 21:34). Martha struggled with this kind of danger. Concerned with providing Jesus comfort, she almost missed out on His gifts to her (see Luke 10:40-42).

Through the words of Jesus, God was giving His very best (see verse 39). Mary perceived this, and sat there listening. What do you do when Jesus is speaking to your heart? Sit and listen? Or fuss with other things? There are so many ways to mask our needs and hide from the voice of our Lord.

Prayer to the Giver

In the prayer Jesus taught, He used *patēr* (Luke 11:2), addressing God in an endearing term that a child would use for his father. Jesus transformed prayer into an intimate experience. Our heavenly Father has greater care and concern for His children than even an ideal human father could ever show.

We do not stand outside God's deeds. Rather He performs His will through human agents. Likewise with His kingdom. God has established and will continue to establish it through His free grace (see verse 2). But the kingdom has no life unless people fill it with obedient and faithful service.

The Lord's Prayer is a prayer to the Giver. He gives material security (verse 3), He gives forgiveness (verse 4). When we in turn refuse others what God has showered upon us, we condemn ourselves.

When a Jewish family retired for the night, they slept close together on mats. Any intrusion would thus waken the whole family. Jesus set this problem over against the hospitality required toward a friend. A friend has come to visit, and a good host must care for him, so the host must look to still another friend for help and wake him up to get the food necessary for the unexpected guest (verses 5, 6).

When something is important enough, we do not hold back, but keep on until it is ours (see verse 8). That is how to use prayer. Later Jesus told the story of the woman who would not give up on her request for justice (Luke 18:1-7). Both stories emphasize the need for continuing in prayer.

The point is not that those who pray must badger God into a reply. He stands always ready to give us what we need (see Luke 11:9). But His choicest gifts go to those who value them most, and to those who understand how they in turn may bless another person.

We know well enough that God does not give everything that human desire imagines. But God does not play bad jokes on us. He does not offer plastic buns when He holds the bread of life in His hands.

Signs Set on Your Way

When the Spirit gives victory and the kingdom rescues another captive, what are we to think? Luke recorded three reactions among the crowd around Jesus:

1. The majority of the crowd was astonished (Luke 11:14). In ancient times it was said when the dumb sing, we would know that the kingdom has truly come. The kingdom continues to surprise us with its victories. But what else should we expect when God is working?

2. Some said that it was Beelzebub, the prince of devils, helping Him (Luke 11:15). *Baalzebub* (2 Kings 1:2) means "lord of the flies"; *Baalzebul,* "lord of the house." It became a common name for Satan. Better any other

explanation than the one that God is working, even if the credit goes to Satan, they decided among themselves.

Jesus rebuked those who would not accept His miracle as the "finger of God" (Luke 11:17-20; Ex. 8:19). What will God say of the sour souls who see only calamity and disaster and never rejoice in the advance of His work?

3. Others said, Show us what else You can do. Give us a sign (Luke 11:16). How preposterous! If the mute who spoke was not sign enough, what would suffice? How can those who demand this or that of the church and its leaders expect satisfaction when they will not accept the evidences of God's power in our midst?

Two kingdoms confront each other in a battle for the control of every life. The person who does not side with Jesus does so with the enemy. He who does not side with the Giver of liberty fights for the captor of souls. The individual who seeks neutrality (see verse 25) has already decided for the evil lord.

Jesus proved Himself the true giver in two ways: His deeds and His words. Both His miracles and His words were signs. But will the world receive them for what they are—evidence that the kingdom is already in operation?

Jesus responded in three ways to the demand for a sign:

1. The cry of the woman (verse 27) set the stage for Him. He cited the queen of the south (verse 31) who had come a great distance to hear Solomon. Now, He asked, what of those who will not hear the wisdom God is giving through His Son? As Jonah proclaimed his message (verse 32), so Jesus did His message of repentance. The prophetic call for repentance is the very sign itself. Nineveh responded. Would Israel? Will we?

2. The urgency with which the queen sought wisdom, and the repentance of Nineveh, witnessed against the Jewish leadership (and all who will not respond). If Israel would not acknowledge the Holy Spirit in the ministry of

Jesus, others (the Gentiles) would. The fact that Nineveh could repent and change reminded Jesus' contemporaries that there was hope for them. There is hope for us, too. But the Son of man will judge all of us (see verse 32).

3. Jesus stated categorically that He was hiding nothing (verse 33). If those who heard and saw did not know what was occurring, they were at fault. The eye that remains clear will see (verse 34). It will discern between light and darkness. Those who have vision blurred with "darkness" (verse 35) will never perceive clearly what God is doing.

If we are at a loss to know God's will, the problem lies with us. When we let prejudice betray our judgment, or spurn the prophetic message, or deny the Holy Spirit His function, we risk our salvation just as much as those who shunned Jesus did.

Locked Away From the Gifts

We can lock God's gifts away from us in many different ways. The woes Jesus uttered against the Pharisees (Luke 11:39-44) show how easily people can cut themselves off from the good things God offers.

When God gives spiritual cleansing, why should we inhibit it with our own ideas of cleanness (see verses 39-41)? The washing the Pharisee expected Jesus to perform (verse 38) had nothing to do with cleanliness. By New Testament times this washing had assumed ritual importance. Religion can too easily degenerate into concentrating on forms.

What a tragedy when God's child dresses up for church, puts on a show, but hides the foulness and taint of sin! As our Lord, God asks of us lives of purity, devotion, and love.

Give away what the cup and the platter contain, Jesus said, and you will receive cleansing from greed and selfishness (see verse 41). Inner cleanliness shows in attitudes toward others. In sharing with others what God has given us we achieve "clean" love for God and neighbor (see verse 41).

Just as God's gifts turn sour when we wrap them with our own forms, so our returning to God what is His due mocks Him if we do not accompany it with changed attitudes (verse 42). Counting out sprigs of mint and parsley has its purposes, but we must above all dispense to others the godly gifts of justice and love.

The Pharisees offered righteousness at a high price in personal performance. If you do not do as we say, you are evil, they implied. Parading their own standards, they affirmed themselves as right by expecting honor for their deeds (verse 43).

The Pharisees feared pollution from unseen or unknown hazards. Hidden graves full of bones (verse 43) made them ritually unclean.

The scribes loved detail (see verse 46), much like lawyers do today. They were preoccupied with small things. They found 39 categories of ways to break the Sabbath. But the church is not a righteousness club. We are not to watch one another in the hope of making others perfectly obedient. Rather, turn your eyes upon Jesus!

When you say that another has sinned and must repent, your task has only begun. Now you must lighten the load, show how God's demand for obedience is met through the provisions of His love and mercy (see verse 46). That the scribes failed to do. Their ancestors had killed off the prophets, and then their descendants saw to it that expensive tombs housed the bodies (verses 47, 48)!

John saw special judgment against those who pierced Jesus (Rev. 1:7). In a contemporary punishment, "this generation" (Luke 11:51) suffered in the destruction of Jerusalem in A.D. 70. By murdering Jesus, they "killed" all the prophets and thus paid the penalty (see verses 49-51).

Worse yet, the scribes took away "the key of knowledge" (verse 52). Guardians of the knowledge of God and salvation must never bury His rule of love and mercy under a growing mountain of regulations and interpretations.

The God who gives all things gave Jesus Christ to save the world. When we offer the world anything less, we are bestowing no gift at all. To give rules, works, or appearances without Him actually robs the world of the gift of life. Instead we must present Him by our loving actions, by telling His words, by living His way, but above all by lifting Him up.

> Give of your best to the Master,
> Give Him first place in your heart;
> Give Him first place in your service,
> Consecrate every part.
> Give, and to you shall be given—
> God His beloved Son gave;
> Gratefully seeking to serve Him,
> Give Him the best that you have.[5]

[1] Joseph A. Fitzmyer, *The Gospel According to Luke*, p. 844.

[2] Eduard Schweizer, *The Good News According to Luke*, p. 177.

[3] J. O. Thompson, "Far and Near the Fields Are Teeming," *The SDA Hymnal*, No. 358.

[4] *The Great Controversy*, p. 484.

[5] Howard B. Grose, "Give of Your Best to the Master," *The SDA Hymnal*, No. 572.

God Cares for Your Life

Luke 12:1-14:35

Years afterward he would still remember what happened. He would never doubt it, for he knew it to be true. Peter had felt Jesus' loving care, had seen it work for him. As a result he penned the words that tell how God looks after us: "Cast all your cares on him, for you are his charge" (1 Peter 5:7, NEB).

Jesus felt the insecurity of His disciples as controversy raged around Him (see Luke 12:4). He sensed their fear if His mission failed. They were so weak; the Pharisees, so entrenched and so sure of themselves. The Roman authorities would hardly protect a small group of "troublemakers" from Galilee.

And were those followers of His any different from what His disciples always would be? Following the beat of the Divine Drummer, apart, out of step with the world, those who truly went His way would always face opposition and misunderstanding.

Why God Says Yes to Us

From the beginning of his Gospel Luke makes it clear that God has said yes to all who trust in Him. If you know you cannot help yourself, and if you let God help you, then saving power is yours. Works righteousness Jesus totally rejected.

Therefore, He said, beware of the mask of the good appearance (Luke 12:1). Not that trying to placate God by good works isn't personally satisfying. The flat dough of your life may feel some stirring as others applaud you or you compare your showing with what others are doing. But the yeast of good works will never make the loaf of your life wholesome. God sorrows when we try that route. He knows the secret sins, the hidden vices.

"As soon as the books of record are opened, and the eye of Jesus looks upon the wicked, they are conscious of every sin which they have ever committed. . . . The seductive temptations which they encouraged by indulgence in sin, the blessings perverted, the messengers of God despised, the warnings rejected, the waves of mercy beaten back by the stubborn, unrepentant heart—all appear as if written in letters of fire."[1]

Together with Christ's righteousness goes His care (verses 6, 7). Jesus gave self-esteem and self-worth to those whom society despised (see Luke 7:37, 47-50). He offers these to everyone who follows Him. You have this great value, this worth, that cannot be calculated.

So many lose faith because they fear that God will reject them. They fear that their badness will repel the God of holiness. But that isn't true. As you say yes to Jesus, God says yes to you (Luke 12:8).

The Bible offers many figures of speech to describe how God saves. We read about justification, redemption, being born again, being grafted into the Vine, sanctification. Do not press the figures of speech too far and too hard. Don't build doctrine on one strand of truth alone. To concentrate on acquittal before God (justification) and neglect the figure of being born again robs us of an essential element that only the rebirth figure gives. And so on.

Brought down to its bare essentials, the saving process has two elements. We say yes to Jesus Christ. He says yes to us. God is the God who says yes to man because of Jesus Christ.

God's care may be most practical: As we stand before authorities, the Holy Spirit will provide us with words to defend ourselves (verses 11, 12), a very real need both in Luke's day and in ours.

Others will so rely on God that they will reject earthly provisions for the future and trust in God's providence (see verses 15-21). The Gettys, the Rockefellers, the Rupert Murdochs, and the Rothschilds of the world have it all wrong. Wealth or position has only short-term security (verse 20).

Near Aylesbury in England, Waddesdon Manor sits astride a hill commanding the valleys around it. In the late nineteenth century Baron Ferdinand de Rothschild built the château to honor his wealth and privilege. He filled it with priceless antiques and art objects. But where is the baron, and will the Son of man say yes to him in the judgment?

Jesus not only acted divine on earth but also pointed to His human nature. He, the Son of man (verse 10), will carry His humanity with Him into the divine judgment and will there acknowledge His followers. His salvation not only operated in Palestine but operates in the here and now, and is carried into eternity. What He does on earth He seals in heaven.

One man could think only of his grievance against his brother (verse 13). Where were his thoughts as Jesus explained God's care? However good the message, however important, minds filled with personal problems may miss God's intent for them. Students of communication call this "interference." Jesus saw this human trait as one of the chief obstacles to faith. "Anxious thoughts" (verse 22, NEB) fill the mind and block the quest for a life of faith (see verses 22-31).

We miss the point if we concentrate in too literal a way on God's promise to provide (verse 28). The clothing we are to seek provides eternal beauty, not earthly protection. The height for which we are to aim calls us to the stature of Christ Jesus.

The unconverted (see verse 29) put their trust in barns and châteaus. They want Paris fashions and gourmet banquets. But we seek robes of righteousness and a place at the marriage supper of the Lamb (see verse 31). The God who knows our needs (verse 30) wants first to answer our greatest lack (verse 31).

Together with God's care comes the kingdom. We confess Jesus, He confesses us and the kingdom is ours. Jesus' "little flock" will receive the kingdom (verse 32). Once again we look back to Daniel, where the saints possess the kingdom (Dan. 7:22).

When asked about her serenity in the face of continual trouble and poverty, an elderly Christian said, "My life may sail the seven seas and be tossed this way and that, but I keep my heart in port." God has given Jesus to be our haven.

But the Christian must turn the coin of salvation over and see what lies on the other side. If the kingdom is engraved on this world through the love of God, so too is the life of the kingdom through the witness and service of the "little flock." While God is caring for us, for whom do we care? For our selfish and sinful needs (verse 45)? Or are we occupied with service for others (verse 42)?

To the crowd (verse 1) Jesus urged preparation for the crisis of belief in Him even then facing them. For us as His disciples the "crisis" would ever be to be faithful in witness and service until the Lord returns (see verse 40).

Jesus showed how much God cares. No earthly master would put a towel around his waist and serve his slaves (see Luke 17:7), but Jesus did for His disciples (Luke 22:27; John 13:4, 5). The serving Christ asks for serving followers. In service we will find readiness for His return. Not just the doorkeeper as in Mark (Mark 13:34) but the whole community of faith (Luke 12:36, 37, 42, 43) will receive the Master's praise for faithfulness and service.

Entering within the circle of God's care may put us in a quandary over how to relate to family and friends (verses 51-53). If they refuse the gospel, what then? Jesus stressed the value of the gospel. Like the Pearl of great price, it demands our all.

I am like a fire (Luke 12:49), Jesus said. John had spoken of fire (Luke 3:17). In scripture fire purifies (Num. 31:23), discerns (Isa. 33:14), and judges (Isa. 43:2). But it also falls on Jesus' disciples. You and I will never be free from the fiery baptism of trial. Just as our Lord went through fierce trial, so do we.

Satan will attack God's people again and again (Dan. 7:25). Yet the kingdom is ours (Luke 12:32). Take care that you are not asleep when the moment for action or the time of crisis or the hour of trial strikes. Jesus gave His warning primarily with His second return in view (verse 40), but it has its message for each and every day.

The prospect of the kingdom (verse 32) means division of the righteous and the wicked. Judgment will fall on the faithless. Therefore watch for the signs of the end (see verse 56). The kingdom will arrive unexpectedly, perhaps sooner than anticipated, but the caring God will provide the faithful with signs of its approach.

This long series of messages from Jesus began with the leaven of the Pharisees (verse 1). It ends on a similar note. All along, Jesus has been urging the right course (verse 57). If you will not put your trust in Christ after all the care God gives you, what hope is there for you (see verse 58)? The question is as timeless as the gospel. The choice is ours. God cares for you, but you must care about His Son.

In and Out of God's Kingdom

Life doesn't always seem fair. Nor is it easy. Good people die when we least expect it, and those who have no regard about others go on and on. Jesus emphasized the need to view reality in the long term. Those who think only of today miss out on the blessings of the kingdom.

But one thing we all should learn. When you see a tragic end to human life (see Luke 13:1, 2, 4) ask yourself one question: If that had happened to me, would I be ready? To perish without repentance is life's greatest catastrophe.

The Galileans, innocently visiting Jerusalem, felt the vicious slash of Roman power and died at the Temple altar. Perhaps going to market or to a party, 18 died when the tower of Siloam tumbled upon them. How like the mindless tragedies filling our news media today!

By *repent* (verses 3, 5), Jesus was inviting His hearers to enter the kingdom of God. He was asking the people to accept His forgiveness, to go and sin no more, and to trust in Him, not the systems men had worked out.

And what of the whole Jewish nation, headed for tragedy? They could read the weather (Luke 12:54, 55) but not the implications of Jesus' ministry or the political path they were treading (see verse 56). The Judge of history would declare against them, and they would pay to the last cent (see verse 59).

The victims of Pilate's vindictive severity and of the unpredictable accident had sinned no more than the nation as a whole. God, the patient orchardist, was losing patience with the unproductive tree of self-righteousness (see Luke 13:6, 7).

In the same way, the institutions of religion face the scrutiny of God. He has no use for those that bear no fruit (see verse 9). And although He waits and waits for our lives to bear the fruits of obedience and righteousness, that patience ends with our death and the judgment.

Those of the kingdom know how to distinguish between compassion and conformity. In rigid conformity to contemporary tradition, the ruler of the synagogue reacted with shock at Jesus' act of healing (verse 14). How barren the branches of legalism!

Compassion must go with joy and praise to the Lord (see verses 13, 17). Obedience in a formal, precise manner will never satisfy the Compassionate One if it overlooks human suffering and need. Jesus distinguished between a life of leaves (see verse 15)—showy but fruitless—and a life of fruit (see verse 16).

Even in the midst of tragedy and selfishness God's grace continues. At times it may seem insignificant, restricted to unimportant people. But watch out, for from that tiny seed will grow a message and a movement that will fill the garden of the world (verses 18, 19).

The world awaits the leaven of the gospel. In Jesus, God placed the yeast of the gospel in the world, and its effect grows ever stronger (verses 20, 21). In Jesus He placed the gospel in your heart—does it grow ever more pervasive in your life?

Why doesn't everyone hear the yes of God? Is the door too narrow (verse 24)? Or are we too loaded with sin and self? Jesus blamed the very people who should be leading the nation into God's favor for blocking the way.

Most scribes of Jesus' day taught that all Israel would eventually be saved. The conditions for that were difficult, but it could and would be done. But not your way, Jesus told the Pharisees and scribes. Your way isn't God's way (verses 25-28).

The paradox of Jesus' teaching is never more dramatic than here. Come to Me, He called, all you who need your burdens lifted; I will do what needs to be done (Matt. 11:28). Yet, at the same time those who seek the way of life must also "strive" (Luke 13:24).

> Come, come, ye saints, no toil nor labor fear;
> But with joy wend your way.

Though hard to you the journey may appear,
Grace shall be as your day.
We have a living Lord to guide,
And we can trust Him to provide;
Do this, and joy your hearts will swell:
All is well! All is well![2]

How true! The loving God is opening ever wider the door of mercy and grace. But the treadmill of life finds us running, yet motionless. Throughout the Gospels, the openness of God's call stands in vivid contrast to our reluctance to break from sin and the world.

The power of grace will not slacken or stop. Where it finds its way barred (see verse 28), it will move on to more receptive hearts (see verse 29). To the horror of many Jews, even Gentiles will sit at the banquet of the Messiah. They will know the value of God's care and accept His invitation.

How easily we may turn aside from God's will for us. But not Jesus. Herod could neither delay nor stop the appointed course of His life (verses 32, 33). Despite Herod's complicity in His death (see verses 31, 32), the power of God, once let loose through the kingdom, would go on healing and curing sinners. God's power is greater than any tyranny or established religion, even when they link hands.

Herod, "that fox," was neither good nor great. Like a fox he was sly, greedy, and crooked. He had neither honor nor glory. Nor more did the leaders in Jerusalem. Like Herod they killed thoughtlessly and ruthlessly. If he sought Jesus' life, did not they likewise? If he stood under condemnation for his execution of John, did not their ancestors for their abuse of the prophets (verses 34, 35) and they themselves for the way they would treat Jesus?

In Luke 9:51 Jesus set His face toward Jerusalem.

Nothing would divert Him from His goal (Luke 13:33). The destiny given by the prophets for God's Anointed He must fulfill. Israel would be stripped of its glory. The Temple itself would stand desolate (verse 35), bereft of the Divine Presence and Power.

A little bit of Herod and the Pharisees lives in us all. We "kill" the prophets by disobeying the Word of God. Our rejection of God's Son will leave us defenseless in the judgment (see verse 35). In that day we will acknowledge Him, but it will be too late. Like ancient Israel, we will have murdered our chances of everlasting life, and will have no hope.

Answer When He Calls

For Jesus to go to the home of a Pharisee (Luke 14:1) showed that neither did the Pharisees exclude Him completely nor did He reject them. Jerusalem boasted several communities of Pharisees, each with strict rules of admission. "The Pharisees were by no means simply men living according to the religious precepts laid down by Pharisaic scribes, especially the precepts on tithes and purity; they were *members of religious associations*, pursuing these ends." [3]

They watched Jesus closely, almost as if He Himself were one of their probationers. Jesus yearned to help the lower classes and took initiatives to include them in His healing ministry. There could be no joy at any banquet when need lingered near (see verses 2-4).

How easy for us to delight in Jesus' teachings and yet miss the point He is making. In trying to hold to what we count as principles or matters of pride, we do not respond in love. God entered that age with new acts of salvation. The joy of the Sabbath should have freed the Pharisee from strict moralism and opened him to the need of his suffering neighbor.

"The Pharisaic communities were mostly composed

of petty commoners, men of the people with no scribal education, earnest and self-sacrificing; but all too often they were not free from uncharitableness and pride with regard to the masses, the *'ammē hā-' āreṣ* who did not observe the demands of religious laws as they did, and in contrast to whom the Pharisees considered themselves to be the true Israel."[4]

The feast at the house of the ruler provided an occasion for Jesus to explain the appropriate attitudes for those who would live the life of the kingdom.

God will exalt those who come humbly to receive from Him (verse 11). (We already know that from the story of Mary and Simon [Luke 7:36-50]. The parables of the lost son and of the rich man and Lazarus [Luke 15:11-32; 16:19-31] will teach it to us again.) Jesus hits at human pride and position because they may satisfy us when we should be seeking the satisfaction He gives.

True humility does not deny self-worth (see Luke 14:11). It keeps it proportioned against the all-surpassing worth of the Lord. With Him in first place, all other positions are inferior. But we need self-worth so that we can value others. Otherwise if we think of ourselves as nothings, then we may regard others the same way.

Nor should we look for reciprocity from our benevolence (verses 12-14). To be generous, to love, without precondition sets us on course in the actions of the new age. In Christ we do not need first place or tenth place, but simply a place. From Him comes all the honor, the identity, the recognition (see verse 10).

Jesus arrived at the house as a guest (verse 1). Where did the host place Him? Scripture does not say. Like us He had to let others rate Him. He frees us from the need to be first always. We do not have to boost our egos by comparing ourselves with others inferior to us. And when we relax in God's care, others can find happiness in our company, just as tax gatherers and sinners found it in Jesus' company.

Later we come to a meal at which Jesus both presided and served (Luke 22:15, 27), was both first and last. He would not have us dominate, but serve. Like Him, we are to open ourselves to all, whether high or low (see Phil. 2:5-11).

How often, in Luke, Jesus used an interruption to move to a new point (for example, Luke 14:15, one of at least 18 times in the Gospel). Thus Luke shifted the story from one subject to another, usually, but not always, related in some way (see Luke 12:13, 41).

Were the guests looking for an invitation to the wedding feast but not with Jesus as their host (Luke 14:16-18)? Did they expect God to act in some other way, provide some other path of salvation?

How minor are our excuses that we offer to the King of kings (verses 18-20)! When we value our goodness or our wickedness or our normality more than we do the Lord, we turn away from the kingdom.

The kingdom demands that we do to others the good that God has extended to us (see verses 12, 13). Jesus encouraged the poor who were now rich in the blessings of His kingdom, and the sick who were now well physically and spiritually, to do for others in accord with how He had acted toward them. Those who answer the call of the kingdom see both their own unworthiness and their own worth. The self-worth that Christ gives now directs us outward to witness, to win, to serve.

God's love claims us totally (verses 25, 26) because divine love will admit no competition. All our love must be in Him, whether toward Him or toward our neighbor. To carry the cross (verse 27) means to live as Christ lived, submissive totally to God's will, committed totally to the welfare of others.

The Lord knows well enough that circumstances

often dictate what happens. The disciple may leave family behind (see verse 26) or may bring them into the faith (see Acts 16:33). Sometimes the way is lonely, and the cross means deprivation (see Luke 14:27). At times we give up all (verse 33); while at other times our property has value in blessing others (see Luke 10:38). The cross each one of us carries may differ from anybody else's.

In this episode (Luke 14:26-33), Jesus teaches us what it means to love Him. He loves without distinction, and cares for all; therefore we will love even our enemies (Luke 6:27). But our love for Him must be so radically different, and greater than our love for anyone else, that the love we have for others appears like hatred in comparison (Luke 14:26). "Nothing between my soul and the Savior."

"He [Christ] assures them [all Christians] that if they take hold of the work with undivided hearts, giving themselves as light bearers to the world, if they will take hold of His strength, they will make peace with Him, and obtain supernatural assistance that will enable them in their weakness to do the deeds of Omnipotence. If they go forward with faith in God, they will not fail nor become discouraged, but will have the assurance of infallible success." [5]

The God of love who cared enough to give Himself totally for our salvation requires total love in return. The total care God gives asks that we care totally about Him. In caring about Jesus and doing His will, we care for others and love them. But that love must never compete with our love for Him or even compare itself with it.

> Here I give my all to Thee—
> Friends, and time, and earthly store;
> Soul and body Thine to be,
> Wholly Thine forevermore. [6]

[1] *The Great Controversy,* p. 666.

[2] William Clayton, "Come, Come, Ye Saints," *The SDA Hymnal,* No. 622. Alt. by Joseph F. Green. Words copyright © 1960 by Broadman Press.

[3] Joachim Jeremias, *Jerusalem in the Time of Jesus,* p. 247.

[4] *Ibid.,* p. 259.

[5] *The SDA Bible Commentary,* Ellen G. White Comments, vol. 5, p. 1121.

[6] William McDonald, "I Am Coming to the Cross," *The SDA Hymnal,* No. 307.

Extravagant Love
—Total Response

Luke 15:1-17:10

Rich and varied figures filled Jesus' speech. He created proverbs and clever sayings so that people would remember the truths He taught. Picking illustrations that showed great contrast, He spoke of the extravagant gesture, of total sacrifice. Once people heard Him, they never forgot His teachings.

The pearl merchant goes out of business to buy and own just one superb pearl (Matt. 13:44, 45)—that's how important the kingdom is. A man "cuts off" his hand, "plucks out" his eye, rather than miss out on eternal life (see Matt. 5:29, 30). A Samaritan merchant empties his purse to help a wounded Jew (see Luke 10:35). A woman wets Jesus' feet with her tears and wipes them with her hair (Luke 7:38, 44).

But such rich figures should not surprise us. Jesus left heaven to come to our world—that is *the* grand gesture. You cannot exaggerate it. Unspeakable gift, immeasurable grace, it reduces the language of extravagance to poverty.

Two Seekers

"Another time, the tax-gatherers and other bad characters were all crowding in to listen to him" (Luke 15:1, NEB). Of course, the Pharisees and scribes came around too (verse 2). The tensions of Jewish society showed in that crowd. The Pharisees and scribes positioned themselves, carefully keeping clear of those tax gatherers and bad characters—clear even of their shadows.

Jesus had no such inhibitions. He delighted as the rejects of religious elitism pressed in on Him. Consequently the complainers misjudged Christ (verse 2)! From their disdainful perches on the edge of the action they *grumbled* or *murmured*. In the Greek Old Testament, that word had come to mean almost one thing only. The prophets used it for Israel when she complained about God's dealings with her, as when the people grew sick of the manna.

When God finally sent the Bread of Life, Israel again complained, even though He brought healing and comfort to the masses. This fellow tolerates sinners. Even eats with them! Ridiculous! Blasphemy! That is not God's way of beginning the kingdom.

Straighten out the sinners first! Get everyone to dress modestly! Insist on the health reform message! And so on. But Jesus never worked that way. Sinners were for saving. And that was where He must begin.

Hidden behind the accusation against Jesus was the ruling of the Law that a son who had become a drunkard and a glutton should be stoned to death (Deut. 21:20, 21). More than once those who finally accused Jesus at His trial tested their evidence in advance (see Luke 7:34).

The willingness of the "bad characters" to listen to Jesus contrasts with the unwillingness of those bastions of self-righteousness and prudery. What would have been our attitude had we been there?

Shepherds, the scribes ruled, could never really purge themselves from ritual pollution because they handled animals continually, and were thought to rob their masters. Women had dubious value as religious examples, despite the scriptural mention of Deborah, Miriam, and others. Yet a shepherd and a woman are the very ones whose desperate search, and exuberant joy upon finding, display God (Luke 15:4-6, 8, 9).

These stories emphasize God's love and mercy and Jesus' call for repentance. God not only "finds" the lost but rejoices in the finding (see verses 7, 10). The parables express in story form what Jesus said in Luke 19:10: "The Son of man is come to seek and to save that which was lost."

The shepherd with his 100 sheep ranked as moderately rich, the woman as pitifully poor, fit representatives of the people crowding around Jesus. Losing domestic animals is a common-enough event. (The goatherd Mohammed edh-Dhib found the Dead Sea scrolls while searching for a lost goat.) The woman in Christ's parable may well have lost one of her dowry coins.

The extravagant joy, and the party that must perforce accompany the invitation to share that joy, stretched both finders' resources. They spent more on the party than the value of what they retrieved! How much God cares!

The scribes had never dreamed of such a thing. In their religion, men sought God. In Jesus' teaching, God actually searches for man!

When God Is Powerless

The parable of the lost son deals with relationships. We read of father and younger son (Luke 15:12, 22), father and older son (verses 28, 31), employer and employee (verse 15), and two brothers (verses 27, 30, 32). It pays to study the story for its message about relationships alone. You can step into the story and find yourself first in the prodigal, then in the older brother, and even in the father.

The parable demonstrates reconciliation. The relationship of a son and his father was restored (verses 20-24). But the same father and another son remained estranged (see verses 29, 30). Jesus' story spells out the steps to reconciliation:

1. The son recognizes that he is in dire trouble (verse 17).

2. He senses a solution through reconciliation (verse 18).

3. He analyzes how he has failed his father (verses 18, 19).

4. He realizes that his father need not receive him (verse 19).

5. He risks all to return to the father (see verse 19).

6. The father is waiting for the son (verse 20).

7. He accepts his son's repentance without quibble or demand (verses 20-24).

8. He does not humiliate the repentant one (verses 21-23).

9. He restores status to the son (verse 22). Many a home would stay together if it showed such openness.

Reasons why reconciliation does not work also appear:

1. The older son explodes in anger (verse 28).

2. He will have no part in the reconciliation (verse 28).

3. He questions his status in the home (verse 29).

4. He rejects his brother (see verse 30).

5. He fails to accommodate the father's provision for the prodigal (see verse 30).

God has the same problems the father had. God's love knows no stint, lack, or condition—it provides for the reconciliation of all. Yet, more often than not, the Father's love fails to reconcile.

The story also shows that in the last analysis God determines the fate of all. The father interrupted the young son (verses 21, 22), refusing to let him talk of hired service (verse 19). He declared the son reconciled and restored (verses 22-24). The father also silenced the older son, declaring in favor of him who remained constant in service (verses 31, 32). God will not fail those who do not fail themselves.

The younger son decided his future by an attitude of repentance and humility (verse 21). The father could provide for the one who could make no provision for himself. The older son made a choice too when he snubbed his father's entreaty (verse 28). The father could not provide for a son who regarded a calf more important than his brother (see verse 30).

This story picks up the theme of "the year of the Lord's favour" (Luke 4:19, NEB). Jesus restored worth and esteem to the poor and helpless (see verse 18). Also, the parable hints at Jesus as the true Elder Brother. Welcoming and making friends of the needy and the outcast, He stood with the Father in embracing them in love. The Pharisees might have brothered the sinners and tax gatherers, but instead despised them and humiliated them.

The two brothers deserved the same fate and for the same transgression. The younger spent the father's wealth, failed to honor his father or provide for him (Luke 15:12, 13), as the Law demanded. The older brother despised his father and rebelled against him (verses 28, 29). One received forgiveness from the penalty through repentance. The other leaves the story with the penalty still against him. The Pharisees doubtless saw through the intent of Jesus' story. How many of them might have also been guilty?

The parable sounds an alarm against—

1. Those who will not help the helpless. Where were the Jews of the Dispersion when the prodigal was in need? The Gentile who provided work (verse 15) at least had some compassion. Those who gave him nothing (verse 16) were the Jews who should have helped.

2. Those who think they can work their way into God's favor. The father would not let the younger son offer service when he needed salvation (compare verse 19 with verses 21, 22). All the effort of the older brother left his sonship in doubt (see verse 29).

3. Those who question the mission of the church as it succeeds among the poor, the ignorant, and the different (see verses 30, 32).

4. Those who refuse their responsibility toward "brothers" (see verse 28).

5. Those who count institutions more important than the saving of a soul (see verses 29, 30).

In one interpretation the three parables in Luke 15 represent the Triune God. Jesus, the Great and Good Shepherd, gives Himself to find the lost. He initiates and takes positive action on their behalf.

The coin of humanity has no power to do or please God unless the Spirit holds it in His power. The Spirit searches, the Spirit finds. Only the Spirit can rescue and give power to the repenting, powerless life.

The Father sent both the Son and the Spirit to search for the lost. The Father waits for the returning ones. The prodigal, like Adam, cut himself adrift from the plans and provisions of the Father. When the sinner returns, like the son, he once more enters the sphere of God's purposes. God welcomes him with exuberant joy.

All is of God, all is of grace, and we rejoice in our salvation. In turn He rejoices in giving it. God is both omnipotent and powerless. For the returning sinner His omnipotence makes up for every lack. But for the refusing sinner He remains powerless. God can do nothing for those who will not accept His entreaties, yet He can do everything for those who respond to His compassion.

> Soul, then know thy full salvation;
> Rise o'er sin, and fear, and care;
> Joy to find in every station
> Something still to do or bear.
> Think what Spirit dwells within thee;

Think what Father's smiles are thine;
Think that Jesus died to win thee;
Child of Heaven, canst thou repine?[1]

The Effort and the Sacrifice

Jesus now considered God's saving act through yet another parable. It asks the question How much will a man do to secure his position in the world of business? How much, then, ought the needy sinner do to secure his position with God?

This parable starts out much the same way as the previous one. Like the son, the steward squandered money entrusted to him (Luke 16:1). And like the son, the steward went over his options, talking to himself (verses 3, 4). In the one story, the son ignored religious scruples to keep alive by tending pigs; in the other, the steward forsook sound business principles in order to survive (verses 5-7).

To the observing business community, the steward was patently dishonest but smart enough to command respect. The solution could work only between rascals: the steward and those who went along with his plot.

The scam worked quite well. It put the master in a difficult position. The Law condemned usury (Deut. 23:19, 20). No Jew could charge interest of a fellow Jew in need. However, the scribes ruled that one might charge it if the person in want still possessed even a small amount of a necessary commodity. If he had a little oil, then he was not "in need," and the lender could charge high interest. The high interest rates made usury very profitable. Oil commanded 50 percent, and grain 20 percent (see Luke 16:6, 7). Thus to avoid interest meant great financial advantage.

If the master sent the steward to jail, the former would confirm that he, the master, was a Law breaker. Yet if he let the steward off, the master would appear weak. But the steward had another thing on his side. In a strongly religious community the master could keep quiet and reap kudos for strict obedience to the Law. The steward was actually making him look good (see verse 8).

The Christian reacts prudently to crisis. He uses his possessions wisely. The manager in Jesus' parable, one of the outcasts of his world, has a message for those who walk the way of faith. We would have nothing unless our Lord gave it to us. Using what we have to God's glory represents good stewardship. At the end we desire the praise of the Master (see verse 10).

"Over and over again a man will expend twenty times the amount of time and money and effort on his pleasure, his hobby, his garden, his sport, as he does on his church. Our Christianity will begin to be real and effective only when we spend as much time and effort on it as we do on our worldly activities." [2]

Mammon (verse 9) means simply "wealth." *Unrighteous* as related to the story would mean "ill-gotten gains." In the concerns of Jesus it would mean possessions accumulated in this "unrighteous" age. God will require an account of how you use them.

The story depicts one rascal benefiting others. In Christian living, the Christian benefits others through the employment of his wealth in service or mission. The companionship of rascals had risked the possessions of the master, while the companionship of the faithful will help ensure eternal security.

Though Jesus spoke various times about the problems of wealth, nowhere do we find that He condemned money as unclean or sinful. How we use our money is what counts. It can curse us or bless us, can curse others or bless them.

The parable does not mean that Christians should use dishonest methods. Those who try to dupe God are fools (see verses 10-12). God knows what they are up to (verses

14, 15).

Luke gives a further note of interpretation. The Pharisees loved money (verse 14). No one can both love wealth and love God (verse 13). The Christian entrusted with great wealth will use it for the benefit of others and the growth of the kingdom. Thus he shows that he serves the Lord, not his wealth (see verse 11).

"Double-minded men and women are Satan's best allies. Whatever favorable opinion they may have of themselves, they are dissemblers. All who are loyal to God and the truth must stand firmly for the right because it is right." [3]

The Law and the Prophets contrast with the good news (verse 16). If the Pharisees had erected barriers (see Luke 15:1, 2), now they tumble as faith breaks down walls of false understanding.

Jesus was not explaining His actions as being the hinge where salvation swings away from the Law and the Prophets to the good news of salvation (Luke 16:16). It is not dispensationalism, as we see when He defined how man comes to God. Not, He said, through the Pharisees' interpretation of the Law, but through the good news that seeks and finds the unworthy and consumes them with its demand for total commitment.

Those who long for the kingdom make the effort and the sacrifice required to win it. Their total response itself echoes the extravagant gesture of divine salvation.

> O love, how deep, how broad, how high,
> Beyond all thought and fantasy,
> That God, the Son of God, should take
> Our mortal form for mortal's sake! [4]

The Despair of Lost Opportunity

Jesus saw the Law as a God-given gift to lead His fellow

Jews to salvation. But by their attitudes the Pharisees distorted the opportunity into impossibility. Had they really heard Moses and the prophets (Luke 16:31), they would have found the kingdom, just as countless of the poor and the outcast had since the preaching of John (see verse 16).

Look, said Jesus, here is an example. Though the law cannot lose its force (verse 17), you twist it so that divorce satisfies your lust (see verse 18). Don't you see that divorce cannot ever be a cover-up for breaking the seventh command?

Moses stated "indecency" as a reason for divorce (Deut. 24:1, RSV). In Jesus' day the Jews were fiddling with the command. Not just adultery, as said the school of Shammai, or perversion, but said the school of Hillel, " 'if she spoiled a dish of food; if she spun in the street; if she talked to a strange man; if she was guilty of speaking disrespectfully of her husband's relations in his hearing; if she was a brawling woman,' which was defined as a woman whose voice could be heard in the next house. Rabbi Akiba went so far as to say that man could divorce his wife if he found a woman who was fairer than she." [5]

The parable of the rich man and Lazarus asks the questions What if you respond totally to the wrong thing? What if you are extravagant with yourself? What if you fail to hear what God is saying about your conduct?

The man of the parable lived in great luxury (Luke 16:19):

1. He dressed in purple and linen. The high priests wore such robes. A laborer would have to work for three years to buy one.

2. He feasted in luxury. The English word best translating the Greek verb would be *gourmandized*. Seeking out costly and exotic foods, he ate things poor people did not even know existed. He frequented the imported food section of the local supermarket!

3. He did this every day. But that wasn't all. He fiddled and gourmandized while lives burned out in hunger (see verses 20, 21).

The plight of the poor in those days reached the same extreme levels that we see in the impoverished nations of the modern world. Poor diet led to poor health. Lazarus did not even possess the strength to drive away the stray dogs that wandered past the estate and with which he sometimes competed for food.

The rich man, completely satisfied with his lot, never thought about helping Lazarus. Like the priest and Levite (Luke 10:31, 32), the rich man passed by on the other side.

The perverse self-assurance of those who totally ignore the plight of others (see Luke 16:25) poses enormous problems for God (see verse 31). The rich man of the parable was not vicious, just stupid. How could he ignore the need at his doorstep? Yet he did and must answer for it—the Christian likewise if he ignores his clear duty toward others.

In the early church God liberated former Pharisees from the attitude here condemned. They joined in helping the poor. The rich gave, opening their tables to those in need (see Acts 2:42).

The tunnel vision of wealth obscures the needy from view. Christ provides peripheral vision so that we may know why He has given us means.

The story has significance only as a parable. To search it for the doctrine of the state of man after death misapplies it and leads to false teaching. If it teaches any doctrine, it is that of Christian stewardship.

"It was not the intention of Jesus to propagate a strict doctrine of rewards and punishment (nothing is said of the piety of Lazarus), or to give a topographical guide to the afterworld. As He tells it, the point of the story is to be found in the character of the rich man and in the reasons for his failure to use the two kinds of opportunity granted

to him, the first by his wealth, the second by his religion
... The two failures of Dives belong together; because his
mind was closed to the revelation of God, his heart was
closed to the demands of compassion."[6]

Faith and Duty

We know that judgment catches up with those who
cause others to lose out (see Luke 17:2). Privilege and
wealth trapped the rich man. The cunning manager
manipulated others to his own advantage. The Pharisees
and scribes, by their attitudes, made the way of salvation
dangerous and tricky.

The New Testament records the deeds of various ones
who set snares for the people of God. Paul wrote Galatians
to meet one such trap. In Acts Paul warned against those
who would deceive and destroy (Acts 20:29-31). Yet we
must distinguish between the deliberate act and the
simple mistake. If a brother offends you and asks for
forgiveness, forgive (Luke 17:3, 4). How often churches
rend themselves apart over the words and actions of one
or more of their members! But Jesus would have nothing
to do with grudge-bearing, revengeful people with long
memories who neither forget nor forgive.

Being human, we find it hard to forget. But when we
remember, we forgive silently yet again. Just as God
forgives us the inadvertent repetition of our besetting
sins, so we forgive the wrongs memory keeps resur-
recting.

Do we have the faith to forgive? Can we keep a watch
on ourselves (verse 3, NEB)? We cannot neighbor one
another without divine help. Nor can we forgive unless
we first accept His forgiveness. The discourse that began
in Luke 15:3 has presented some hard things to accept.
How right to pray, "Increase our faith" (Luke 17:5)!

"The disciples, faced by the demand for unlimited
readiness to forgive wrongs, see that this needs a great

amount of faith; so ask that their faith may be increased. . . . The saying is a paradox of the same kind as the camel passing through the eye of a needle. Neither the one nor the other is meant to be attempted in the literal sense. . . . The word of Jesus does not invite Christians to become conjurers or magicians, but heroes like those whose exploits are celebrated in the eleventh chapter of Hebrews."[7]

How do we relate to Christian duty (verse 10)? Do we seek credit for fulfilling it? Do we want to be noticed? Do we expect a divine pat on the back—if not now, then later? The Pharisees numbered their good deeds, but the Christian never seeks an edge with God.

In a previous parable Jesus told of the master who girded himself and served his servants (Luke 12:37). That did not happen in real life, except with Jesus. Now we are back living real life. No servant expects service from his master, but rather more tasks to do. Thus with the Christian. Look to the duty God commands, Jesus says, not the rest when it is over.

God never holds back anything in His saving quest, not even sparing His own Son (Rom. 8:32). He acts with extravagant love to provide more than we need. Like the father of the prodigal, He restores us and then adds a status we never had before.

For us this means total response. It boggles the mind how the Pharisees and scribes measured and counted, dickered and dealt. This must not be so in My kingdom, Jesus said over and over again. Love acts in total response to the need it sees, just as God totally acted in our favor. For this we need faith.

Lord, increase our faith.

---

[1] Henry F. Lyte, "Jesus, I My Cross Have Taken," *The SDA Hymnal*, No. 325.

TGWSY-7

[2] William Barclay, trans., *The Gospel of Luke*, The Daily Study Bible Series, p. 208.

[3] *The SDA Bible Commentary*, Ellen G. White Comments, vol. 5, p. 1086.

[4] Thomas à Kempis, attrib., "O Love, How Deep, How Broad," *The SDA Hymnal*, No. 148.

[5] Barclay, p. 212.

[6] G. B. Caird, *Saint Luke*, pp. 191, 192.

[7] T. W. Manson, *The Sayings of Jesus*, p. 141.

Time Runs Out on Choices

Luke 17:11-19:10

Luke told of 10 lepers Jesus healed (Luke 17:12-16). Just one returned in thankfulness. Nine Jews had a chance to confess their Deliverer, but only a Samaritan did.

Like a parable, the 10 lepers represent needy mankind. Salvation says yes to all. Only the ones who say yes to Jesus gain wholeness. The Samaritan received salvation, not the nine Jews (see verse 19).

When the man came to Jesus, he had already been cured. In many other stories, healing and faith in Christ intertwine so that the one seems dependent on the other. Not here. A healing miracle is not the same as salvation itself. What the person does with the miracle counts (see Luke 12:8, 9). Nine accepted the miracle but did not acknowledge Jesus (Luke 17:17, 18).

"O give thanks unto the Lord; call upon his name: make known his deeds among the people. Sing unto him, sing psalms unto him: talk ye of all his wondrous works" (Ps. 105:1, 2).

When the Choice of Faith Runs Out

In the fierce days of trial that precede the coming of the kingdom, at least three false paths have the potential to destroy faith:

1. *A false emphasis is placed on times and seasons.*
Will perfect obedience to the will of God bring Christ

back? If Israel kept two Sabbaths perfectly, that would be enough to bring the Messiah, some Jewish leaders taught. But the kingdom does not come "with observation" (Luke 17:20). Concentration on the timing of the coming of the kingdom is not to be our concern. Prepare, rather, for the power of the Spirit, who will give authority to our mission. (See Acts 1:6-8.)

How often faithful church members dwell on timing and faith suffers! Someone will develop a bevy of Bible texts and Ellen G. White quotes and use them to set out what the church must do before the Lord will return. Or will employ them to prove that the Lord will appear either at a specific date or within certain time limits.

Here are a few of the proposals some took seriously in our recent history:

a. The year 1964 must be a key date in the Lord's plans because Noah warned the world for 120 years. The Adventist warning message has gone out for nearly 120 years, so watch out for 1964!

b. All of us have marks and scars of sin. In the final atonement Jesus will remove them. When we receive the final atonement the Lord will have a prepared people, and Jesus will come. In the early sixties, some who followed this approach were claiming complete freedom from sin.

c. April 22, 1984, will mark the beginning of the last three and one-half years of the present age. Jesus will return at its end.

And so we might go on. Such arrant nonsense ought never seduce us. Yet some have lost their faith this way. One group, deeply impressed by a theory like those just given, turned away from the witnessing that had dominated their Christian experience. Looking inward, they sought spiritual perfection and tried to live sinless lives. They even separated themselves from society, forming a small commune in a secluded forest where they lived on a "translation diet."

When they were finally convinced that they were following utter foolishness, most returned to church. Now, however, they took no part in missionary service, criticized the other church members, and showed a decidedly negative spirit.

"The days of the Son of man" (Luke 17:22) filled one small corner of the earth with joy and deliverance. To think that this human theory or that set of teachings or this series of events will create those marvelous moments at *our* wish denies God His freedom (see verses 22, 23). The frenetic search for new days of power has robbed many of faith. We will know Him in power and glory on "his day" (verse 24).

"Above all, disciples are not to be misled by bogus prophets trying to declare the signs of the times or to indicate the time and place of the revelation. Jesus makes it clear that the arrival of the Son of Man will be sudden and unmistakable; it will not require other human beings to call attention to it."[1]

2. *Indifference deals faith a deadly blow.*

While some chase exciting theories, the blahs of life hypnotize others of us. Time goes on. Nothing appears to happen. We turn to the world and let its interests rule us. Faith dies.

Noah knew better and warned his world. But they wouldn't take any steps for their own salvation (verses 26, 27). Lot knew better but ran the risk. Only a special act of God rescued him (see verses 28, 29). Unthinking, indifferent humanity will suffer judgment. Nonchalance may be the pattern, but the circumstances demand unceasing alertness.

"The Redeemer of the world declares that there are greater sins than that for which Sodom and Gomorrah were destroyed. Those who hear the gospel invitation calling sinners to repentance, and heed it not, are more guilty before God than were the dwellers in the vale of Siddim. And still greater sin is theirs who profess to know God and to keep His commandments, yet who deny Christ in their character and their daily life. In the light of the Saviour's warning, the fate of Sodom is a solemn admonition."[2]

"The most dangerous of all theological errors is that which says, 'He's a good fellow, and 'twill all be well,' rashly assuming that our indifference and carelessness have their counterparts in heaven and that God's holy purpose must inevitably come to terms with our shallow optimism."[3]

3. *It is thought that God will accept almost any lifestyle.*

Possessions delude and destroy (see verse 32). The Western world settles in comfort, and finds faith hard to come by. The poor of the world, denied possessions and even enough food, seek the Lord's provisions and discover saving faith.

Sharing the same activity does not guarantee salvation. God will not hesitate to separate the faithful from the faithless (see verses 34-36).

What did Jesus want us to understand about the future? "The essence of it is that the existing world-order based upon selfishness is the exact contrary to the kingdom of God. The economic structure of society, the social organizations, the political methods of the nations—these things flatly contradict all that Jesus means by the kingdom of God. Therefore they are doomed to perish. . . . He [Jesus] regarded the times and seasons as something which God kept in His own hands. For Jesus and His disciples the immediate and urgent business was the service of the kingdom."[4]

Jesus showed that time would elapse between His ministry and His coming, though recent attempts to rewrite Adventist interpretation of prophecy have taught otherwise. It has been claimed that Jesus expected the kingdom at once after His resurrection, or in a few years, and that no room exists in the teachings of Jesus for the long time periods of the year-day principle of interpretation of prophecy.

Such an idea requires the reinterpretation of plain words so that some of what Jesus said is claimed to be original and some to be additional words added by the Gospel writers to make room for the passing years. But such reasoning destroys the basic unity and authority of the Word.

God Wins and Loses as Faith Meets the Test

The story of the persistent widow continues to reflect on the disciples' prayer "increase our faith" (Luke 17:5). It also answers the important question What kind of faith does God ask as His children wait for vindication? The parable is for those living in anticipation of the coming of the Son of man (see Luke 18:1).

Herod, and at times the Romans, appointed paid magistrates who lived well off bribes. Justice came only to those who could afford to buy it. "Officially they were called *Dayyaneh Gezeroth*, which means judges of prohibitions or punishments. Popularly they were called *Dayyeneh Gezeloth*, which means robber judges."[5]

How difficult it can be to penetrate the barriers of officialdom and the bureaucracy. "Have you an appointment?" "He's at a meeting." "His secretary will see you." "Come back tomorrow." "What was it you wanted to see him about?" The padded excuses are intended to fend us off, but the desperate grow more and more persistent.

A widow would have no money for a bribe, but people would observe her coming day after day. The judge feared for his reputation. *Weary me* (verse 5) carries the meaning of "give a black eye" or "spoil a reputation."

The behavior of the judge bears no relationship to God's way of dealing. Like the widow, we remain in communion with God and do not give up. Unlike the judge, God knows and cares (verse 7); He is already saying yes to those who show faith. He will avenge them, He will put the record straight, He will show His favor toward them (Dan. 7:22; Luke 22:29).

No period of time is too long when God, the faithful judge, is on our side. While the comment of Jesus (Luke 18:8) points us forward to the Second Coming, the vindication of God arrives with our confession of Jesus as Lord (see the following parable).

"Jesus is speaking of the certainty of speedy action when the time comes. When He asks whether the Son of man will 'find faith on earth,' he is not suggesting that there will be no believers. He is saying that the characteristic of the world's people at that time will not be faith. Men of the world never recognize the ways of God and they will not see His vindication of His elect."[6]

Of God Jesus asked, "Will he delay?" (verse 7, RSV). Christ's followers, like the widow, persist in prayer. They pray constantly, not because God will not answer or does not care to answer, but precisely because He does answer and does care. God will have a people of faith (Rev. 14:12) in the last days. Patience, or persistence, is one of their traits of character.

God vindicates, or avenges, His children (Luke 18:7), a theme that links the two parables at the beginning of chapter 18. Another common factor that links them is prayer. The petition of the widow was persistent (verse 5), while the prayer of the tax collector was humble (verse 13).

Twice in Luke Jesus used the aphorism about those who exalt themselves being humbled (Luke 14:11; 18:14). The Pharisee had so loaded his prayer rocket with self-congratulations (Luke 18:11, 12) that nothing could lift it off the ground, let alone orbit it to the courts of glory.

The tax collector, meanwhile, had stripped himself of

self-importance and was lean and hungry for righteousness. He had no merits to qualify for a place in God's kingdom, but perhaps he might receive God's mercy (verse 13).

It would be nice to believe that justification by comparison died out with Jesus' parable. Alas, not so. Christians who know better hope that God will deal on a comparison basis.

The Pharisee had a place for all those whom he thought inferior. Tax gatherers, adulterers, and extortioners must keep to their place, and that certainly wasn't where he was! Modern cultures also speak of those of another culture as "having their place." That place isn't where they are, nor is it as good or as valuable. However, a world church has no room for such arrogance and foolishness.

The pious may appear better than the sinful. In the parable, conceit and contempt of others contrast with unworthiness and guilt. The one who flies to God, not to boast, but to confess, has His mercy.

"It is one of the marks of our time that the Pharisee and the publican have changed places; and it is the modern equivalent of the publican who may be heard thanking God that he is not like those canting humbugs, hypocrites, and killjoys, whose chief offense is that they take their religion seriously. This publican was a rotter; and he knew it. He asked for God's mercy because mercy was the only thing he dared ask for." [7]

Jesus continued to talk about the various tests that faith must meet. Seeming delay has its answer in persistence. Great need has its fulfillment in God's grace. Now Jesus explains yet again.

He showed concern for children far different from the normal disciplinary and severe attitude. Fond of children and interested in them, He affectionately mentioned a game of theirs (Luke 7:32), delighted in their hosannas, and spoke of the witness of babes and sucklings (Matt. 21:15, 16). Now He both called children to Him and used them as a model for true Christian faith (Luke 18:16, 17).

"Let mothers come to Jesus with their perplexities. They will find grace sufficient to aid them in the care of their children. The gates are open for every mother who would lay her burdens at the Saviour's feet. . . . Let not your un-Christlike character misrepresent Jesus. Do not keep the little ones away from Him by your coldness and harshness."[8]

Jesus, Friend of little children, be a Friend to me;
Take my hand and ever keep me close to Thee. . . .
Never leave me, nor forsake me, ever be my Friend;
For I need Thee from life's dawning to its end.[9]

Even little children may respond to the call of Jesus and share His favor and His kingdom. If it can be theirs, it can belong to all, especially as we follow their example of trust and desire.

It isn't who you are, it's what you are. Are you a person of position (a ruler, verse 18)? You still must come in humility and ask, "What shall I do to inherit eternal life?" And if you give the "right" answer (see verse 21), the one your culture demands of you, the one that has backing from religion—then you may not yet be what you should be (see verse 22).

Like the Pharisee earlier on in the chapter, the ruler who came to Jesus has his sources of security. Jesus never spoke of riches as dangerous, rather of rich people who are in danger because of their being rich (verse 24).

Throughout His ministry Jesus had to struggle to break the hold of a view that equated God's approval with conformity and prosperity. He sought to strip away false security. It wasn't enough to have wealth and the praise of others, nor was it enough to conform in morality and religiosity (see verse 21).

What went wrong? The ruler saw relying on God as really relying on nothing. It was too intangible. Where were the houses and lands? Where the investments and precious metals? The other things he felt one could depend on? Only radical renunciation of dependence on such things sets the stage for one to be a disciple. We remember Barnabas and Zacchaeus, who gained through the use of their wealth for others. In modern times we respect Mother Teresa of Calcutta for surrendering any worldly comfort for the benefit of others. If this young man had reacted differently he would be remembered differently.

You cannot drive a truck and trailer through the door of a doghouse. Nor can a camel shrink itself enough to go through a needle's eye. A rich man may find equal difficulty with the narrow door that leads to life (see verses 24, 25). Jesus pointed to the power of God that can accomplish what no earthly security ever can (verse 27).

Riches themselves do not bar the way to the kingdom. Lack of surrender does. The Spirit guides the surrendered heart in knowing what it must forsake. God says, Trust Me. Hear My yes. Then, we will discover, all things are possible (verse 27); even the rich person may learn to lean on God and not on his wealth.

But how much the human heart longs for rewards. Hear Peter speak for all the poor in spirit who seek the kingdom: "Lo, we have left all, and followed thee" (verse 28). What should we expect? How much will God give us?

"Even Peter does not understand; he thinks that he and his fellows deserve better than the rich ruler because they have made the sacrifice at which he balked. Whimsically Jesus promises that those who have left home and family for the service of the kingdom will find themselves caring for a far bigger family than the one they left, before ever they reach the eternal life of the age to come." [10]

God protects us from knowledge that might destroy our faith. Would the disciples have gone to Jerusalem with Jesus had they understood His fate (verses 31-33)? And if they had not gone could they have ever really known the great price paid for man's shame and guilt? Or shared the wonder of the Resurrection?

Our minds have protective filters. We do not hear what we don't want to hear (see verse 34). At times the bad news of our sin never really registers. Nor do we heed the counsels of righteousness. But life is no game of let's pretend. Right now or around the corner lurk trials and temptations of which the Spirit is warning. Will our minds close out the Guiding Voice?

Choosing God's Way

Luke likes to remind us that Jesus fulfilled prophecy (see verse 31). A beggar in chapter 18 corrects those who interpret Jesus' identity wrongly. When he is told, "Jesus of Nazareth," the perceptive blind beggar declares, "Thou son of David" (verses 37, 38). In a Negro spiritual the poor of the world of slavery position themselves with Bartimaeus:

> When I fall on my knees,
> With my face to the rising sun,
> O Lord, have mercy on me. [11]

The storyteller in Luke wants us to know the man's desperation. The first word for cry (verse 38) describes someone calling in a loud voice to attract attention. Hearing the crowd starting to move off, he feared Jesus might ignore him or not hear him for the rabble. His voice now rose to a yell, a scream, an ungovernable shout that demanded Jesus' attention (verse 39). Lord, his whole being cried, say yes to me!

When Jesus comes near through the Spirit, do we cry "so much the more, Thou son of David, have mercy on me" (verse 39)?

The man who begged his neighbor for bread (Luke 11:5-8), the widow who kept after the judge (Luke 18:2-5), and this blind petitioner remind us again and yet again that prayer for divine blessing must never stop. Not because God gives in at our nagging, but because our prayer has brought us to the faith and dependence necessary so that God may safely do for us what we seek.

Don't fall silent, don't hide your desperation, when you need Jesus. Your friends, your relatives, and even your pastor may fail to hear your longing cry, but Jesus is already saying yes to you.

Luke throughout his book speaks often of "the people," using the Greek word *laos* more than any of the other Gospel writers. Luke uses it 19 times between Luke 18:43 and the end of his Gospel. In the Septuagint, *laos* means "the people of God." Luke contrasts "the people" with the rulers of the people.

The multitude singing and shouting the glories of the Son of David lacked one thing. They did not understand or accept the cross (see verse 34). How often people movements claim Jesus as their inspiration, their "guru," but never can be Christian because they have no cross.

In a radical rethink of the divine purposes, Jesus had moved salvation away from the community and nation to individual response (see Luke 19:1-10). No longer could the seeker position himself to advantage among the redeemed nation (see Luke 10:25). His personal response to the initiatives of God would be crucial.

The story about Zacchaeus sums up a number of points:

1. The gospel reaches to all, including tax collectors

and sinners (see Luke 19:2, 3).

2. God has taken the lead in the drama of salvation (verse 5).

3. Human response to God's initiative requires a discipleship that devotes everything to the mission of the One it follows (see verse 8).

4. Though Zacchaeus had a right to salvation, saving action occurred only because Jesus went after him and sought him out, not because of who he was (verses 9, 10). So it is with us.

Jesus' willingness to accept creates joy now as then. Going with Zacchaeus to his house meant not only fellowship but also forgiveness. The Jews in general regarded a tax collector as a sinful man. To stay or to eat in such a person's house gave the guest a share in his sin. Thus Jesus removed Zacchaeus' guilt, even as He does ours.

In his response Zacchaeus went far beyond the expected. The rabbis recognized 20 percent of one's wealth as a suitable provision to make recompense. Fifty percent was unheard of. Zacchaeus applied to himself the penalty applied to sheep rustlers (Ex. 22:1; see 2 Sam. 12:6). In voluntary restoration, the Law only required repayment plus one fifth (Lev. 6:4, 5). Repentance showed itself by the extent of the restitution. The repentant sinner responds to the great value of the gift of salvation.

---

[1] Joseph A. Fitzmyer, *The Gospel According to Luke*, p. 1167.

[2] *Patriarchs and Prophets*, p. 165.

[3] T. W. Manson, *The Sayings of Jesus*, p. 144.

[4] *Ibid.*, p. 148.

[5] William Barclay, trans., *The Gospel of Luke*, The Daily Study Bible Series, p. 222.

[6] Leon Morris, *Luke: An Introduction and Commentary*, pp. 263, 264.

[7] Manson, p. 312.

[8] *The Ministry of Healing*, pp. 42, 43.

[9] W. J. Mathams, "Jesus, Friend of Little Children," *The SDA Hymnal*, No. 543.

[10] G. B. Caird, *Saint Luke*, p. 205.

[11] "Let Us Break Bread Together," *The SDA Hymnal*, No. 403.

How to Prepare for the Future

Luke 19:11-21:38

The precautions appeared overwhelmingly detailed and careful. The countdown went as planned. But the preparation proved tragically inadequate. Not much more than one minute after blast-off the *Challenger* shuttle exploded in a ball of flames. In the reviews and inquiries that followed, the meticulous preparation proved flawed.

How are we preparing for the interstellar journey God will provide His people? What a tragedy if, at the very moment of triumph, our inclusion should be aborted, our preparation inadequate.

In explaining the approaching end, Jesus sets one parable against another. Be ready for the sudden and unexpected coming of the Son of man, He commands (Luke 12:39, 40). Concentrate on witnessing until that time, He also tells us (see verses 42, 43). Obviously He saw no problems in mixing the two apparently contradictory directives. We keep our faith in Him strong as the tension between watching and witnessing fixes our attention on Christ and His purposes for us and the world.

Knowing What Is Important

If we think that it is structure and institution that make up the kingdom of God—if that is where we express our faith most fluently—we are little better than the rulers of the Jews. The one who prepares for the eternal future knows that the kingdom of God is within him. It will survive and triumph whether or not the trappings of a successful and growing movement surround him.

The parable of the 10 pounds (Luke 19:11-27) spotlights two groups: the servants of the nobleman, and the citizens of his country. The servants represent the church at any time in history; the citizens symbolize the Jewish leaders of that day in particular, and in general all those who organize against God's plans.

When we let the kingdom message do its work, God's plan marches on (see verses 15, 17). The servants have worked, but the pound has multiplied itself (verses 15, 16, 18). Like the leaven (Luke 13:20, 21) and the mustard seed (verses 18, 19), the kingdom has God's power.

To use the pound wisely is to witness. The 10 pounds added to the one doesn't mean that we have more commands to obey, but that we witness even more to the kingdom.

In the parable, the "far country" (Luke 19:12) equals a long time, not great distance. Again our Lord opened the possibility of an unknown period of time between the Ascension and the return.

The parable of the ten virgins (Matt. 25:1-13) concerns judgment, as does this one. The final judgment puts every Christian to the test. Though the punishment of the rebellious is gruesome (Luke 19:27), the parable emphasizes the point that the judgment will divide. All who do not survive the test will meet the second death.

"What matters is the faithfulness that is revealed in action (verses 15, 17). The disciples have left their possessions; in the community they find their new home, above all at the consummation (Luke 18:28, 30). The blind man cries out to Jesus and then follows Him (verses 38, 43). Zacchaeus leaves his villa and goes to those of whom he has taken advantage (Luke 19:3, 8). The act itself is not salvation—the enemies are very active (verses 14, 27)—but is the act of a disciple who knows that, like a child, one is totally dependent on God and opens oneself to God (Luke 18:31-34). This is precisely what Jesus Himself will do in the Passion narrative, pioneering the way for His disciples."[1]

When the moment comes for prophecy to be fulfilled, God will provide everything needed (cf. Zech. 9:9 with Matt. 21:1-7 and Luke 19:29-35). The Mount of Olives figures in a significant Old Testament prophecy (Zech. 14:4). The King riding on a colt (Luke 19:35) reminds us of the time of Israel's growing power (1 Kings 1:33).

Because the Pharisees accompanying Jesus had long since taken sides against Him (Luke 19:47), they voiced their displeasure (verse 39) at the joyous noise and confusion surrounding Him. But nothing could hold off the praise (verse 40) to God's Messiah as He came to Jerusalem, the Temple city. Jesus put Himself at center stage. At the end every eye will see Him (Rev. 1:7). Just so, at the entry to Jerusalem He came most publicly, as the King (Luke 19:38).

Tears fell for what would one day happen to the city of God's peace (verses 41-44). He saw the Roman armies, the heedless slaughter, the defiant rashness. If only . . . He cried. The tears fell, too, for a beloved nation that found it impossible to accept God's messengers—the reproofs they gave and the divine plan they outlined.

The "if only"s of history have as much to do with individuals as with cities and nations. Jesus' tears reflect all the needless pain and suffering caused through rebellion against God.

Jesus took control of the Temple (verses 45-47). Isaiah defined the purpose of the Temple (Isa. 56:7), and Jeremiah described what it had become (Jer. 7:11). Because only Tyrian currency could be used in the Temple, money changing was big business. A trade in animals for sacrifice made the precincts more like a cattle market than a temple. Money changers and animal traders deliberately victimized the Temple patrons. God never approves of worship that exploits the worshipers.

When the holy and good are misused or profaned, what do we do? Do we permit our Lord to drive out compromise and evil from the life? Have our "temples" become a house of prayer, inhabited by the Holy Spirit, or are they places where we barter with sin and trade with the devil?

When Religion Goes Wrong

A religion that fears to speak the truth (Luke 20:5, 6) has no future. Spineless preachers who will not rebuke sin, or fail to submit their people to the authority of God's law, have no place in last-day faith.

The people had already heard John, a true prophet; now they listened to Jesus. Throughout His ministry, questions about the Baptist continued. John's great influence carried on into the apostolic age (Acts 19:1-7).

A religion that refuses God's messengers (Luke 20:9-15) has no future. Jesus showed great concern about stewardship. What we do with God's gifts and God-given opportunities we shall be held accountable for in the judgment.

In those days the leaders did not hear the prophets, not even John the Baptist (verse 5). Do we heed the latter-day messenger of the Lord? To us from an ancient servant of God comes the counsel "Believe his prophets, so shall ye prosper" (2 Chron. 20:20). In believing and obeying the prophetic messages we prosper in the faith.

Jesus' mind swept back to Daniel's great prophecy of the stone that filled the earth (cf. Luke 20:17, 18 with Dan. 2:34, 35). Systems of thought, whether personal, national, or religious, that will not confess the Son will be wiped out. Beyond the cruel fate awaiting the Son of God (Luke 20:13-15) will come the day when God will act to vindicate

His name and cause (verses 17, 18).

A religion that marvels and does nothing (see verse 26) has no future. The constant tension between Jesus and the rulers brought some notable interchanges. Once before, they had sat amazed at His intelligence and wisdom (Luke 2:46, 47). Some 20 years had passed, and Israel's leaders had learned little from the Divine Wisdom among them.

Luke calls us away from the fantasies that would create the kingdom of God through political or military endeavor. Caesar has his authority (Luke 20:25), but so also does God. The way of the cross will lead the disciples to victories and powers that Caesar cannot imagine (see Luke 17:25; 19:10).

The Romans levied a poll tax on each adult Jewish male every year. Jews resented it because it reminded them of Rome's rule. They had to pay it with the silver coin stamped with the emperor's head. Because they objected to images on religious grounds, the coin was universally hated (the day-to-day currency did not bear Caesar's image).

"Nothing speaks more eloquently of the robust quality of His [Christ's] mind than His ability, in the momentary exchange of controversy, to enunciate a principle which has proved to be the basis of all future discussion of the problem of church and state (cf. Rom. 13:1-7; 1 Peter 2:13-17)." [2]

We cannot completely untangle the secular and the sacred. God, in part, deals with man through the structure and order of human society. Human governments, as long as they remain within their function of providing order and system to society, have a right to expect their due. Caesar, however, has no right to lay claim to what God demands—our absolute and complete obedience to His will.

A religion that denies the resurrection (Luke 20:27-40)

has no future. The Sadducees probably descended from the Zadokite priests who staffed the Temple (see 1 Chron. 6:6-10). By Jesus' time they included both priests and lay aristocrats. Josephus said that the wealthy followed them but that they had no hold on the people.

Generally the chief priests were Sadducees. They feature largely in Acts (Acts 4:1; 5:17; 23:6-12). "The patrician families of Sadducees formed a tightly closed group, with an elaborate tradition of theology and doctrine; they kept strictly to the exact text of Scripture, which shows the conservative character of these circles." [3]

The levirate marriage described by the Sadducees (Luke 20:27-33) ensured procreation on behalf of the male line of a particular family. To the Jew procreation dominated the purposes of marriage. They had limited concepts in areas such as companionship, marital love, and fulfillment of the wholeness of man and woman. Because Heaven provides eternal life the demand for children to preserve a particular line falls away.

"Jesus gave them [the Sadducees] an answer which has a permanently valid truth in it. He said that we must not think of heaven in terms of this earth. Life there will be quite different, because *we* will be quite different. It would save a mass of misdirected ingenuity, and not a little heartbreak, if we ceased to speculate on what heaven is like and left things to the love of God." [4]

A religion that seeks human solutions to eternal issues (see verses 41-44) has no future. Though Jesus fulfilled the requirement of Davidic descent (Luke 3:31), He rejected the implications of the scribes. Despite what they taught, the Messiah would not sit on an earthly throne, ruling Israel and the nations.

The Jews played games with the interpretation of Psalm 110 (verse 1 quoted by Jesus in Luke 20:42, 43). In Jesus' time they regarded it as Messianic. When the

Christian church used it to prove that the Messiah would be the Divine Redeemer, the Jews rejected this application, applying it instead to Abraham. Later, when the church and the Jewish faith had gone their separate ways, they restored the original interpretation! How careful we must be that our understanding of Scripture is not too conditioned by a temporary condition of the church.

A religion of show and self (Luke 20:45-47; 21:1-4) has no future. Ambition and love of privilege drive some leaders to arrogant and cruel acts. In contrast with display and selfishness, Jesus' life demonstrated self-lessness and humility. He must ever be our model. Love like His sets an example that advances the kingdom of Heaven.

The gift of the widow (Luke 21:1-4) had much value because it matches in spirit the gift of the Son of God. God did not spare His own Son. The widow did not spare her all. If Heaven gives His All, what may we withhold?

Standing Firm at the End of Time

Jesus announced the coming end of the world, reckoning on a considerable and indefinite interval before the end (verses 8-19, 25-28). Also, He showed the clear distinction between the coming destruction of Jerusalem and the end of the world (verses 20-24).

Though the memory of the destruction of Solomon's Temple rankled in Jewish minds, they regarded Herod's Temple as a considerable and permanent structure. Some of the building stones (see verse 5) measured as much as 45 cubits in length (about 66 feet). Among the gifts to the Temple was Herod's golden vine with clusters of grapes said to be the height of a man.

The scribes and chief priests were already plotting the destruction of Jesus and His work (Luke 20:19, 20). He predicted not just a Temple wrecked, but the building stones of Jewish faith pulled asunder.

The temple of faith is the church, "which is his body" (Eph. 1:23). The One the Jews and Romans would raise on a cross at Calvary would build the new temple through His sacrifice, while at the very moment of that sacrifice the significance of Herod's Temple would come to an end, with the ripping of the inner veil (Luke 23:45). The shell would survive nearly another 40 years, but the body of Christ will carry the church to the temple of God in the new earth (see Rev. 21:22).

Jesus' preliminary remarks filled His disciples with alarm (see Luke 21:7). When will this destruction happen? How will it happen? they asked. Jesus showed more concern for faith than for a timetable of the future:

1. *False claims may snatch away our faith* (verses 8-11). Jesus had already warned of this (Luke 17:22-25). How often through the centuries someone has misled sincere believers by claiming special knowledge about the timing of Christ's return. How many have come saying they are Christ.

Jesus creates a time line with the caution signs "the end is not yet" (Matt. 24:6; cf. Luke 21:9), "before all these" (Luke 21:12), "the times of the Gentiles" (verse 24), and "when these things begin to come to pass" (verse 28). Time would pass by before the destruction of Jerusalem (verse 20). And still more would go by between then and the coming of the Son of man (verse 36).

How long? How many years? We do not and cannot know. But we can and must preserve our faith (verses 34-36).

"Thus Luke agrees with Mark in stressing the certainty of the end, but showing that it would not happen immediately after the resurrection of Jesus and that, although 'signs' might be seen, it would be impossible to forecast when it would take place. Further, the thrust of both discourses is paraenetic [exhortatory] rather than apocalyptic. Jesus is not concerned to impart apocalyptic secrets to the disciples, but to prepare them spiritually for what lies ahead."[5]

2. *Persecution and mocking from unbelievers may wear out our patience* (see verses 12-19). Jesus emphasizes endurance as one of the key features of people of God. They survive through divine help (verses 14, 15). But their loyalty will enable them to witness before the most important people (see verses 12, 13). Jesus laid the foundation for this view of persecution and trial in the Beatitudes (Luke 6:22). Just as the prophets made the most of it when tormented and outlawed, so should they. In fact, Jesus said, "On that day be glad and dance for joy" (verse 23, NEB).

Confrontation as occasion for witness is a biblical theme. The one who "shall wear out the saints of the most High" (Dan. 7:25) wants to stifle witness. We must never remain silent under pressure, Jesus said. Steadfast endurance does not really harm us, but assures us of the resurrection (see Luke 21:18, 19). The evidence against Satan and his cohorts mounts steadily as he leads the attack on faith.

3. *The disarray of established systems and beliefs gives certainty to the prophecies of the end* (see verses 20-24). Jerusalem filled the cup of iniquity by its persecution and murder of the prophets (Luke 13:34, 35; 20:9-16). Just after Jesus' birth, Simeon hinted at the results of wrong national choices (Luke 2:34). His townspeople threw Him out (Luke 4:29). Jesus alludes to Hosea 9:7 as He speaks of the days of vengeance (Luke 21:22), and to Deuteronomy 28:64 as He predicts captivity (Luke 21:24). Thus what was written will be fulfilled (verse 22).

"The Saviour's prophecy concerning the visitation of judgments upon Jerusalem is to have another fulfillment, of which that terrible desolation was but a faint shadow. In the fate of the chosen city we may behold the doom of a world that has rejected God's mercy and trampled upon His law. . . . The world will then behold, as never before, the results of Satan's rule."[6]

The destruction of modern Babylon parallels Jerusalem's fate. If the bulwark of Judaism, which sheltered God's truth, was about to crumble, what fate will God bring upon the great whore (Rev. 18:21-23)? Babylon will lie plundered and desolate for the same reason as Jerusalem: she has murdered the prophets and God's people (verse 24).

In Paul's little apocalypse he saw the destruction of those who deny and oppress the truth (2 Thess. 2:10). Babylon of Daniel's time and Jerusalem of the apostolic age shared a similar fate and give a similar message: God will destroy those who destroy His people and His truth. What happened to those two cities will happen to all who oppose God (Rev. 20:10, 15).

4. *The prospects of the final liberation bring continuing cheer and confidence to God's people* (Luke 21:25-28). Jesus began His ministry by proclaiming liberty (Luke 4:18); now He announces the ultimate yes as God delivers His people and establishes the eternal kingdom. Throughout His teaching, Jesus has referred to Himself as the Son of man. For the world the prospects of His coming cause terror (Luke 21:26). For the redeemed they bring relief and joy (verse 28).

Jesus foretells two types of signs. He brings forward those about nations in conflict (verse 10), and later speaks of nations in perplexity (verse 25). The continual warmongering of national entities yields to the horror of international politics out of control. Also, He points to evidences in the natural world. The earthquakes and famines (verse 11) escalate until nature herself goes out of control (verses 25, 26).

Every political crisis, each war, each flood, every earthquake, heralds the coming of the Son of man. Each has the quality and substance of the very things that will happen with ever greater intensity as the Second Coming nears.

> It must be time for the waiting church
> To cast her pride away,
> With girded loins and burning lamps,
> To look for the breaking of the day.
>
> O it must be the breaking of the day!
> O it must be the breaking of the day!
> The night is almost gone,
> The day is coming on;
> O it must be the breaking of the day! [7]

A reservoir of evil waits to flood the world (Rev. 13:1, 11-18). All that withstands it are the Lamb and His faithful followers (see Rev. 13:8; 14:1). The coming of the Son of man on a cloud (Rev. 14:14; Luke 21:27) averts the flood and destroys its power forever.

When the whole earth threatens to fall apart, that is the very hour of deliverance. The worse conditions are, the more likely the time is almost here. At that bewildering hour when the world holds nothing that is reliable or safe, Christ appears with His new order. The old order breaks down, the new order breaks in. For this blessed hope Jesus commands us, Look up, rejoice (Luke 21:28).

5. *There can be no doubt that these things will happen; Jesus the Lord says so* (verses 29-33). Like many trees, fig trees are bare during winter, shooting forth new leaves in the warming spring. Just so comes the end. The turbulence of the last days, like winter, will give place to the radiance of the coming Sun (see Mal. 4:2).

While this parable has its primary application to the

approaching end (Luke 21:29-31), it also hails the summer of salvation in which all who will may awaken to new life (see Luke 7:22). The sap of eternal life already flows. The Saviour of the world has come.

In what sense will "this generation" see "all . . . fulfilled" (Luke 21:32)? Both verses 32 and 33 have a similar message. Jesus' words about the Temple had their fulfillment, and His words concerning the coming of the Son of man will surely have their fulfillment. This generation can be sure that what He said is already under way and will come to the prophesied end. The thrust of the statement is directed at those who might scoff at Jesus' words. What this generation will shortly witness is part of the whole of God's purpose. Once on the way, it is as good as accomplished, and this generation will witness it happening.

The passage has problems if we look for a particular generation who will see all these things. It wasn't true of those to whom Jesus spoke, except in the sense that some of those then living will be raised to see Christ return (Rev. 1:7). Nor will it be true of the Jews as a nation, because prophecy no longer makes them its special focus. To push the statement forward to the generation that will see Christ return avoids the intent of the statement, however true it may be that they will comprehend all that appears in Luke 21. The emphasis is on certainty, not on a time period.

6. *The watchful and the ready will stand before the Son of man* (verses 34-38). With such evidences to testify to the coming events, and with the surety of Jesus' words, the followers of Jesus must stay always alert. Jesus explains what that means. He is not talking about careful analysis of prophecy and charts of last-day events, however important and helpful they may be. Nor is He referring to doctrinal correctives and human guesses about the reason for delay. Instead He calls us to prayer (verse 36), to

spiritual watchfulness (verse 36), to holy living (verse 34).

Our status is assured (verse 36) provided we continue in prayer and overcome the temptations of life. Jesus stands as judge (see verse 36). Those who "escape all these things" (verse 36) are not like those who fled to the mountains as Jerusalem was about to fall (verses 20, 21). *Escape* here means going through the temptations and trials of the last days with faith still intact.

"Are the people of God now so firmly established upon His word that they would not yield to the evidence of their senses [when Satan personates Christ]? Would they, in such a crisis, cling to the Bible and the Bible only? Satan will, if possible, prevent them from obtaining a preparation to stand in that day. He will so arrange affairs as to hedge up their way, entangle them with earthly treasures, cause them to carry a heavy, wearisome burden, that their hearts may be overcharged with the cares of this life and the day of trial may come upon them as a thief." [8]

For the last time "all the people" (verse 38) hear the voice of their Saviour. Soon—too soon—He will face His tormentors. Luke closes this portion of his story with Jesus teaching large crowds.

What began in Bethlehem will continue to the coming of the Son of man. "The year of the Lord's favour" that Jesus proclaimed (Luke 4:19, NEB) knows no December 31. Though the calendar pages flick past one by one, His yes still holds. His salvation still calls us to a new life.

---

[1] Eduard Schweizer, *The Good News According to Luke,* p. 296.

[2] G. B. Caird, *Saint Luke,* p. 222.

[3] Joachim Jeremias, *Jerusalem in the Time of Jesus,* p. 232.

[4] William Barclay, trans., *The Gospel of Luke,* The Daily Study Bible Series, pp. 250, 251.

[5] I. Howard Marshall, *The Gospel of Luke,* p. 754.

[6] *The Great Controversy,* pp. 36, 37.

[7] G. W. Sederquist, " 'Tis Almost Time for the Lord to Come," *The SDA Hymnal,* No. 212.

[8] *The Great Controversy,* pp. 625, 626.

Innocence and Guilt

Luke 22:1-23:48

Even now I remember my protestings. Despite what the teacher claimed, I had not done it. I was innocent. Isn't it curious how the mind captures forever wrongs suffered, yet cannot remember all the escapades for which one was truly guilty?

Remember Jesus the innocent. No wrongdoing, no sin, ever recorded against Him. The conscience of the world fell silent the day He died. Humanity—you, me—nailed Him to the tree: a shameful and odious deed. As Jesus perished, a Roman centurion declared, "Beyond all doubt, . . . this man was innocent" (Luke 23:47, NEB).

A scheming, callous establishment sought His death. "The chief priests and the doctors of the law were trying to devise some means of doing away with him" (Luke 22:2, NEB). Do we by our lives still try to "do away" with Him? His death is meaningless to you without your confession of Him.

Jesus Entrusts the Kingdom to His Followers

The plot to destroy Jesus had begun long before (John 5:16). He knew what fate awaited Him, but those plotting His death did not realize that they were channeling His life toward resurrection, as well as death (Luke 9:22).

Jesus' death grants a new status for the forgiven. Mary found forgiveness (Luke 7:44-50). The father wrapped his lost son in the robe of righteousness (see Luke 15:20-24).

And Jesus does the same for each person who accepts Him.

The Pharisee gloried in his status with God but had none, while the tax collector despaired of his spiritual condition and found God's mercy (Luke 18:11-14).

Key texts in Luke's Gospel teach the following:

1. Humanity is in a desperate plight (Luke 4:18; 7:47).

2. Mankind needs repentance (Luke 3:3; 15:13-18; 19:8, 9).

3. Jesus seeks for the lost (Luke 5:31, 32; 15:3, 8; 19:10).

4. The suffering of the Son of man leads on to glory (Luke 9:22, 51; 22:29, 30).

5. Judgment awaits the sinner (Luke 19:20-24; 21:34-36).

6. Because of Jesus, God acknowledges the repentant (see Luke 10:20).

In the cross God embraces our prodigal world with saving love, but that very act drives off a second world that, like the elder brother (Luke 15:25-30), spurns that love.

The suffering and death of Jesus (Luke 9:30, 31; 20:14, 15) represented the will of God. He "must" suffer (Luke 9:22). Jesus fulfilled prophecy through His suffering (Luke 22:37; 24:25-27). But it was not just the compelling will of God, He also poured out His blood "for you" (Luke 22:20). Christ suffered, and so must the church (Acts 14:22). Through the suffering of Jesus, God saves; while through the suffering of the church, salvation reaches out to the world.

He lived among outcasts and He died with them (Luke 22:37; 23:33). Even in His death He sought and saved sinners (Luke 23:43, 47). His death opened up the certainty of saving power for all who repent.

"Luke, then, sees three things. (1) Jesus' ministry, which consummates the fate of the Old Testament prophets, is a road to suffering, deliberately taken . . . (2)

This effects salvation in Jesus' love for humankind, thus (3) making possible the post-Easter way of service and suffering taken by the community. But just as in Revelation 5:9 only Jesus is the lamb that has purchased a people for God, so for Luke, too, Jesus' Passion remains the absolute foundation for all later experience."[1]

In Jerusalem the longing of the people for Jesus delayed the ultimate scheme of the rulers (see Luke 22:2). But Satan did not give up (see Luke 4:13). The satanic fifth column infiltrated and betrayed the cause of Christ (Luke 22:3, 4).

We are not immune to Satan's deceptions. Judas' understanding of prophecy led him to suppose that Christ would have to preserve His purposes at all costs. We may be terribly wrong as Judas was.

Had Judas mulled over the defection of the rich young ruler and how much that had cost Christ's movement? Why, the disciple may have wondered, had not Jesus directed some of Zacchaeus' surplus cash into the money bags that he held? System, institution, and investments would no more secure God's mission then than they will now!

Satan has tied puppet strings to every life. The gospel frees us. But the devil does not give up. Even after Judas had been with Jesus three years, the deceiver had the disciple dancing at the end of a string. He wants you there, too.

Betrayal continued. To argue over position (Luke 22:24) betrays Jesus. To hold back witness (verse 34) betrays Him. But betrayal of our Lord need not be the end. Jesus gave the kingdom to the disciples (verses 28-30), and Peter recovered his position of trust (verses 60-62; John 21:15-17).

History has too many similar stories that tell us how quickly and happily men will betray their positions of trust when they perceive gain. Yes, even within the church itself.

How far man lives from God's intentions! At the very moment when we should come closest to Him our humanity stops us short and we look to self (Luke 22:24; 1 Cor. 11:18-20). Once before, James and John had tried to jump the gun and get ahead (Mark 10:35-40). The One who is totally giving Himself must deal with envy and jealousy among His closest followers. Why do we ever ride the world of self, drifting further and further from God?

In an amazing show of what it means to receive God's yes, Jesus confirmed the gift of the kingdom (Luke 22:28-30) to His quarreling colleagues. Yet the gift of the kingdom cannot secure us from danger. Judas yielded to greed, and Peter succumbed to pride and fear.

Jesus prayed for Peter with eternal consequences in mind (verses 31, 32). The future needs those who survive temptation and failure through the power of Christ. Beyond our mistakes new possibilities emerge. In Jesus Christ we do not yet know who we might become, where we might be led, what we might do.

If we think we can protect ourselves against trial we will fail as Judas and Peter did. Our arms can never win the battle of the Lord. In sorrow Jesus said, "Enough, enough!" (verse 38, NEB). Not that two swords were enough—or any number of swords, for that matter—but that they had not understood, and to go on talking in this vein was profitless.

Through periods of great joy and fellowship and sad treachery and misunderstanding Jesus prepared Himself for the sacrifice He must make. From the gospel story we learn about love, we learn about weakness. If love finally gives us the kingdom, it will be because of the God who seeks and saves—not because of who we are and how well we perform.

Luke features Jesus' concern about the faith of the disciples. He taught them how to pray (Luke 22:40), urged upon them faith that would endure. Tests approach continually. The Father's strength will protect us as it did Jesus.

Any day, every day, may raise terrible obstacles to our faith and endurance. What will we do? Deny our faith like Peter (verses 56-60)? Remain constant to God's will as did Jesus? And if we fail, will we have the humility and good sense to know that failure, as for Peter, may be a way station to greater service?

The Old Testament links the imagery of the cup with suffering and with the wrath of God (Ps. 11:6; Isa. 51:17; Eze. 23:33). Judgment would fall against the sinner in whose place He now prepared to die. Would it strike Him? For His sinless nature, the responsibility of the awful sin He would bear produced the fierce agony of Gethsemane.

A site at the foot of the Mount of Olives provided an often visited retreat for Jesus. In this visit to the Garden of Gethsemane, Jesus found the serenity and strength, as He communed with His Father, to go through with His sacrifice for humanity (see Luke 22:42, 43).

Had there ever been a scene such as this? The Saviour of the world in agony in the garden? Jesus' mission hung in the balance at this point (verse 42). He might have turned back, given up. But in the victory of that hour, He lent to you the power to do right, to submit to God's will.

What language shall I borrow to thank Thee,
    dearest friend,
For this Thy dying sorrow, Thy pity without end?
O make me Thine forever; and should I fainting be,
Lord, let me never, never outlive my love to Thee.[2]

Jesus prayed, "Thy will be done" (Matt. 26:42). What prompted it? What motivation can lead a person to utter such a statement?

1. It may be said when one is held helpless by an irresistible power—hope gone, despair in control.

2. A person may have been battered into submission—victory out of the question, defeat accepted.

3. He may say it out of utter frustration, as of a dream that can never come true—regret, anger, bitterness, filling the soul.

4. Or he may say it in perfect trust. Jesus trusted His Father, said yes to the divine purpose. Submitting to the love and care of His Father, He made the hardest of all decisions and accepted an outcome He could not at that moment perceive—submission, trust, hope, rested fully in God.[3]

"With the issues of the conflict before Him, Christ's soul was filled with dread of separation from God. Satan told Him that if He became the surety for a sinful world, the separation would be eternal. He would be identified with Satan's kingdom, and would nevermore be one with God."[4]

With the angel at His side, "he prayed the more urgently" (Luke 22:44, NEB). However much He had pleaded for strength a few moments before, anguish now flooded Him. The word *agony* appears only once in the New Testament. Luke searched his Greek vocabulary to find this word. It conveys the intensity of the struggle as He fought against terror and fear of the future. In a vivid image Luke describes the physical effect of His suffering: "Like clots of blood" His sweat fell to the ground (verse 44, NEB).

The disciples were "worn out by grief" (verse 45, NEB). The most stringent test awaited them. Prayer would see them through even as it preserved Jesus' determination to fulfill God's purposes. Nothing anywhere in the Bible says more about the need for prayer and the power it possesses than this episode.

When Darkness Reigns

The father had kissed the prodigal (Luke 15:20) in love and restoration; Mary had kissed Jesus' feet (Luke 7:38) in joyful gratefulness. Now Judas debased the common courtesies of greeting and turned the kiss of welcome into betrayal (Luke 22:47, 48).

But Luke will not let us forget the cosmic value of this event. The Son of man, to whom God has given the kingdom, refused the power that He might have seized as rightly His, and permitted Judas' tawdry trick.

Now the dark power had his way (verse 53). In the flood of truth that spilled out as Jesus taught in the Temple, darkness found no footing. But with the lying kiss of Judas, and in the isolation of a midnight garden, Satan, the liar, began his final assault on Christ. From now on until the Resurrection, darkness reigned.

Jesus has "rescued us from the domain of darkness" (Col. 1:13, NEB). What happened at the cross affects the entire universe. The forces of Satan seemed in control, but Christ won a glorious victory. Even now as we wrestle against the kingdom of darkness (Eph. 6:12), victory may be ours.

If we sent our Lord to the cross, then we also are Peter hiding away from the shame and threat that event brings (see Luke 22:54-60). Later Paul would speak of the cross making Jews stumble and Greeks ashamed (1 Cor. 1:23). Only true faith can cry with the apostle, In the cross of Christ I glory! (Gal. 6:14). Yet even in that shout of victory, the child of faith knows that Peter's weakness lurks in his own heart, waiting to deny its Lord yet again.

If two of His closest associates would betray Him and deny Him, what might He expect from His enemies? The mocking, persecuting, physically violent assault now began (Luke 22:63-65).

"There were two main stages. First, there was a Jewish

trial in which the chief priests had Jesus condemned according to the Jewish law and then tried to work out how best to get the Romans to execute Him. Then a Roman trial followed in which the Jewish leaders prevailed on Pilate to sentence Jesus to crucifixion. The Jewish trial was itself in two or three stages. During the night there were informal examinations before Annas (as John tells us) and Caiaphas (who had some of the Sanhedrin with him). After daybreak came a formal meeting of the Sanhedrin. This was probably an attempt to legitimate the decisions reached during the night."[5]

Jesus had spoken of the sufferings He would endure (Luke 9:22; 17:25). They now began. Arrested, beaten, blindfolded, mocked, misunderstood, He was now the suffering servant of Isaiah 53. "He is despised and rejected of men; a man of sorrows, and acquainted with grief: and we hid as it were our faces from him; he was despised, and we esteemed him not" (verse 3).

Luke brings together various titles used of Jesus: (1) Prophet (Luke 22:64, NEB); (2) Messiah (verse 67, NEB); (3) Son of man (verse 69); (4) Son of God (verse 70); (5) I AM (verse 70); (6) Christ (Luke 23:2); (7) King (verse 2). Who some thought He might be, or who others accused Him of claiming to be, He in fact is.

How often we refuse to accept the full power of the Lord. Do we want Him as the Lamb to take away our sins, but not as the Lord to rule our lives? Or accept Him as the Son of man, sharing our identity, but deny Him as the Son of God, wielding divine authority? Or receive Christ anointed for God's purposes but refuse Him as the King who controls our destiny?

Crucify Him!

No Roman court would have anything to do with a charge of blasphemy. Three times the Jewish leaders turned to the accusation of subversion (Luke 23:2, 5, 10).

How strange! They accused Him of fomenting the very thing in which He refused involvement (see John 18:36). He would not lead a national political revival. Their charge was patently false. They knew it, and Pilate perceived it too.

"Three times he declares Jesus innocent; but three times is twice too many; what should have been a single, authoritative, and final decree becomes first an argument, then a losing argument. The decline and fall of Pilate begins when he hears that Jesus comes from Galilee and tries to shift responsibility on to Herod Antipas." [6]

Jesus remained completely silent in the presence of Herod (Luke 23:9). The two Roman officials found solidarity in their dealing with the King of kings (verse 12), just as the rulers of the earth will in their opposing Him at the end (see Rev. 13:3, 4). Herod thought Jesus fit only for contempt (Luke 23:11). How often men have decided that way about Jesus! But at the last day the contemptible becomes the conqueror (see Rev. 19:11-16).

This Man Is Innocent

Luke adds new dimensions to the story of the cross by giving us material no other Gospel writer includes. We know Jesus to be the Son of man, the king of Daniel's prophecy (Dan. 7:13, 14). Those who have made judgment against Him will themselves meet judgment (see Luke 23:29, 30).

"The women lament the fate of Jesus. They raise the death wail over Him in anticipation. He in His turn raises, as it were, the death wail over Jerusalem in anticipation. The Holy City is doomed, and those who weep for Jesus might well weep for themselves if they knew what the future held in store for them." [7]

Peter speaks of judgment that begins at the house of God (1 Peter 4:17). A similar idea appears in Jesus' saying about the green and dry trees (Luke 23:31). If crucifixion proves the fate of One who was three times declared innocent, what will happen to those guilty of His death? Fire destroys dry wood, and may even consume green trees (Eze. 20:47). The cruelty of man against man may fail to measure innocence, but the guilty are more certain to suffer.

Only a few hundred yards lie between Pilate's palace and Calvary. But the time line stretches through eternity. Jesus is "the Lamb slain from the foundation of the world" (Rev. 13:8). Simeon saw the cross as a sword piercing Mary's heart (see Luke 2:34, 35). Jesus knew that a cruel death awaited Him (Luke 9:22). On the Mount of Transfiguration, Moses and Elijah talked with Jesus about "his departure," (verse 31, NEB), meaning the cross. Before He would return to heaven He must go to Jerusalem (verse 51); He had "a baptism to undergo" (Luke 12:50, NEB); as a prophet He must perish at Jerusalem (Luke 13:32, 33); He must "suffer many things" (Luke 17:25); He would be maltreated and killed at Jerusalem (Luke 18:31-33); the leaders "sought to destroy him" (Luke 19:47); the son in the parable of the wicked husbandmen died at their hands (Luke 20:9-15). Finally, He was counted among the transgressors (Luke 22:37).

Luke wrote his Gospel with the cross in view. Jesus moved toward it. However the road wound, the cross was His goal. Because we know it to be His fate, Luke treats the actual event with quiet, reverent simplicity (Luke 23:33).

For all who hung Him there, Jesus prayed forgiveness (verse 34). Their ignorant cruelty would repeat itself in the death of Stephen (Acts 7:59, 60; see Acts 3:17; 13:27). That they slew an innocent Man was wrong enough; that they shared in killing the Son of God was a deed unimagined. We know who He is because we have evidence, but do we accept what intellect and senses tell us?

Who are we as we picture Him dying for our sin? The greedy soldiers squabbling over His clothing (see Luke

23:34)? The rulers mocking at His apparent inability to save Himself (verse 35)? The crowd watching, wondering What next? The Roman soldiers rejecting the One who would bring light to the Gentiles (see verse 36)? It matters greatly what we do with the crucified Christ.

The world divides before Him. The multitude drifts to death, spurning the sacrifice, questioning God's purpose, looking elsewhere for hope (see verse 39). But some see through the moment of loss to the victory waiting ahead. All realize that they must pay the price of sin, but some find eternal life because they recognize that Jesus is able and willing to accept sin's guilt and grant pardon, and they ask (see verses 41-43).

Death need not snuff out the gift of eternal life. "You shall be with me in Paradise" (verse 43, NEB) carries the assurance of everlasting life in our Lord.

" 'Today' refers not to 'the calendar day of the Crucifixion' (E. E. Ellis, *Present and Future*, p. 37), but to the day of 'Messianic salvation inaugurated by' the death of Jesus. The criminal will share the kingly condition of Jesus that very day."[8]

If we speak of the cross and mean more than the rough-hewn timbers, what do we mean by the nails that pinned Him to the wood? The thief found his answer. Have we found ours?

Palestine lay shrouded in darkness when an unseen hand desecrated the Temple and its worship (see verse 45). "Luke may well be suggesting in his own way what the Epistle to the Hebrews does more explicitly (Heb. 9:26-28), that by the death of Jesus access to the intimate presence of God has been made possible for human beings, even those not serving the priestly courses of old. Similarly, it may be Luke's way of expressing what the Epistle to the Ephesians calls the 'dividing wall of hostility' between Jew and Greek (Eph. 2:14-16, RSV), broken down 'through the cross.' "[9]

Jesus died serene, at peace and forgiving. A tortured nature and sympathetic witnesses attended His death (see Luke 23:45-47). Luke does not say with Mark that He died as "a ransom for many" (Mark 10:45) or with Paul that He was "put to death for our trespasses" (Rom. 4:25, RSV). But make no mistake. He died the Saviour of the world. Unknowingly, in their taunts the rulers spoke the truth: He is God's Messiah, His chosen (Luke 23:35). He is the king of the world, not just of the Jews (verse 38). He can and does forgive (see verses 34, 43). And He is innocent (see verse 47, NEB).

"Well, then, might the angels rejoice as they looked upon the Saviour's cross; for though they did not then understand all, they knew that the destruction of sin and Satan was forever made certain, that the redemption of man was assured, and that the universe was made eternally secure. Christ Himself fully comprehended the results of the sacrifice made upon Calvary. To all these He looked forward when upon the cross He cried out, 'It is finished'" (John 19:30).[10]

---

[1] Eduard Schweizer, *The Good News According to Luke,* p. 340.

[2] Bernard of Clairvaux, attrib., "O Sacred Head Now Wounded," *The SDA Hymnal,* No. 156.

[3] See William Barclay, trans., *The Gospel of Luke,* The Daily Study Bible Series, p. 272.

[4] *The Desire of Ages,* p. 687.

[5] Leon Morris, *Luke: An Introduction and Commentary,* p. 317.

[6] G. B. Caird, *Saint Luke,* p. 246.

[7] T. W. Manson, *The Sayings of Jesus,* p. 343.

[8] Joseph A. Fitzmyer, *The Gospel According to Luke,* p. 1510.

[9] *Ibid.,* p. 1514.

[10] *The Desire of Ages,* p. 764.

Wait for
the Power

Luke 23:49-24:53; Acts 1:1-26

A soft mist drizzled onto Regent Street in London. It was Christmas. Along the streets crowds waited for the Prince of Wales to turn on the power for the holiday decorations. Suddenly laser beams of green, red, and orange divided the darkness. The mist became a marvel of iridescence as the shafts pierced the concrete valley between the stores and bent their brilliant rays into Oxford Street.

At the foot of the cross one group stood apart. They watched and waited. We read in the Bible of the bewilderment and fear of the disciples (for example, see Matt. 26:56), but little about hope. Yet Luke would not have them wailing and beating their breasts like the people (Luke 23:48). This group were witnesses (verse 49)—the waiting yet uncommissioned church.

And so for us. With the cross in focus, with the Innocent dying for us, making us dead to sin, we await new life from our loving God. The Power from on high and the glory of the kingdom lie ahead. From the cross, shafts of light pierce the darkness of time and place.

They Remember His Words

Like Simeon and Anna (Luke 2:25, 38), Joseph of Arimathea looked for the kingdom of God (Luke 23:51). As in the stories of Simeon and Anna, the story of this godly, expectant believer points to a future that will now unfold.

The story is far from over, a new beginning awaits us. Again the devout gather around Jesus. This time He is not a babe, but the crucified.

Joseph came from "a city of the Jews" (verse 51). The women whom Luke previously mentioned in his gospel (Luke 8:2, 3) came from Galilee (Luke 23:49). Both the respected Jew and the humble women served Jesus in different ways. Because of Joseph, Jesus lay in a new, unsoiled tomb (verse 53). The women would continue their service of love for their Lord despite His death (Luke 23:55-24:1).

Luke 23:54-24:1 defines the edges of the Sabbath. The day of preparation (Luke 23:54) is Friday, the day before the weekly Sabbath (Mark 15:42). The dawning of the Sabbath announces the arrival of the holy day (see Luke 23:54).

The women who had followed Jesus from Galilee have a message for us: Guard the Sabbath and keep it holy.

Beyond this Sabbath (verse 56) lay the Resurrection, the Ascension, the church, and the consummation of all things. On that Sabbath the turmoil and conflict ceased. The trusting rested, and so did their Lord. Then when the Sabbath was past, God would begin a new work created through the death of His own dear Son.

In different ways, at different places, the New Testament poses the question How will you react to the resurrection of Jesus?

1. *Some were "utterly at a loss"* (Luke 24:4, NEB). Caught up in the law of cause and effect, they had no explanation for what they saw.

When your senses deny the truth about God and yourself, what will you do? How should you react?

Scripture gives two answers. First, believe the heavenly witness. "He is not here, but is risen" (verse 6). Second, remember the word of the Lord. Jesus had said, "The Son of man must . . . be crucified, and the third day rise again" (verse 7).

Two heavenly witnesses assured the women at the tomb that their eyes did not deceive them. But the wonder of angels would pass, and men wouldn't believe (verse 11). You can trust something else: "Remember how he spake unto you" (verse 6). To their own eyes they must add the witness of the word.

2. *Others regarded the telling of the event to be an idle tale* (verse 11). In legal matters the Jews thought two, and at the most three, witnesses enough. But women were dubious as witnesses. Did such chauvinism lie behind the failure of the disciples to accept their testimony (verses 10, 11)? Gossip, not fact, came from female lips. At least that was the common wisdom.

It serves the writer well that the apostles still would not accord women credibility. Their role was not forgotten but surfaces in Acts as women accomplish great things for God (for example, Acts 9:36), and in an Epistle of Paul's as he sweeps away sexist barriers (Gal. 3:28).

Can life with Jesus really be as good as He says it will be? Are the promises of God truly yes in Jesus Christ (2 Cor. 1:19, 20)? Even peering into the experience of others or going to see what good thing has happened may not be enough. The apostles thought the women spoke nonsense. Peter left the tomb amazed but unconvinced (see Luke 24:12).

"While the Saviour was in God's presence, receiving gifts for His church, the disciples thought upon His empty tomb, and mourned and wept. . . . Their unbelief in the testimony of the women gives evidence of how low their faith had sunk. The news of Christ's resurrection was so different from what they had anticipated that they could not believe it. It was too good to be true, they thought."[1]

Hearts on Fire

Two disciples finally became aware of who was with

them (verse 31). At first they did not recognize Him (verse 16). Not that we should look for sinister causes. "Satan is not involved, but mere human incredulity reigns. Before the veil is removed from their sight they have to be instructed. . . . Finally, they come to recognize Him, not by seeing (looking at Him), but with the eyes of faith, in the breaking of the bread. So He is finally made manifest to them—and He vanishes."[2]

What was it that kept those disciples from knowing Jesus? Not the setting sun, even though Emmaus lay west of Jerusalem. Nor their downcast eyes, even though they had reason enough to mourn. Luke makes the reason clear. They could not know Jesus because they were slow to believe what Scripture said about Him (verse 25). The thought of Him being alive had not registered, despite the witness of the prophets, despite the testimony of the women, despite Jesus' own predictions.

Could we be as dull and slow to believe as they were? If you want to "see" Jesus, examine what the prophets say of Him (see verse 27). Know Him first from the Word of God, and then your view of Him will be truly enlightened (see verse 31).

At another time, in another setting, Jesus said, "If any man hear my voice, and open the door, I will come in to him, and will sup with him, and he with me" (Rev. 3:20). The Laodicean invitation finds its roots in experiences such as the one at Emmaus. Jesus, the most courteous of guests, awaits our invitation. What if those two had said goodbye to Him at the door to their dwelling? Jesus will enter, bless, and reveal Himself to us if we invite Him (see Luke 24:29-31).

In the house where the two ate with Jesus, they thought Him guest, but He served them as host (verse 30). When we invite Jesus into our lives He serves us with the bread of life. We are forever His guests, and He forever the provider.

Have you trod your Emmaus road and known your Lord? On May 24, 1738, John Wesley had his journey. He writes: "In the evening I went very unwillingly to a society in Aldersgate Street, where one was reading Luther's preface to the Epistle to the Romans. About a quarter before nine, while he was describing the change which God works in the heart through faith in Christ, I felt my heart strangely warmed. I felt I did trust in Christ, Christ alone, for salvation; and an assurance was given me, that He had taken away *my* sins, even *mine*, and saved *me* from the law of sin and death." [3]

"And so the reader is asked where he or she stands along this road; among the perplexed, with whom Jesus nevertheless journeys; among those who reflect and listen to questions, who have heard what others have to say, who allow their hearts to be moved by Scripture, who cannot escape and refuse simply to put an end to their disquiet; or even among those whose eyes have been opened in table fellowship with the risen Lord, so that they can find the road to others." [4]

Of Jesus the Bible says, "He is the Yes pronounced upon God's promises, every one of them" (2 Cor. 1:20, NEB). Only as He is seen that way can the journey from Emmaus to the needy world begin.

The fire of conviction sent the two men scurrying back to Jerusalem and the other followers of Jesus (Luke 24:33). Now their witness could join that of the women. Here the church has its true origin. The fellowship of believers grows only out of a conviction that Jesus lives and serves them still (verses 34, 35). In witness to each other was born the impetus to witness to others. For this reason too, even today, in testimony meetings, by casual conversation, in sermon and lesson, we share our common experience of the Lord and find ourselves driven to witness.

Total conviction about the risen Lord had not yet settled in the hearts of the disciples. The Lord had walked to Emmaus with two witnesses, and had appeared to Simon Peter (verse 34). What was for some academic but amazing suddenly became reality. A Form appeared, a voice spoke (verse 36). They shook their heads, covered their eyes, cowered away, thinking they had seen a ghost (verse 37).

The Resurrection did not cancel the Crucifixion. We feel the otherness of the resurrected One as He appears and vanishes at will. His is a power that we cannot comprehend. Stephen would glimpse Him at the right hand of God (Acts 7:55). John would view Him with angel hosts and the full array of the courts of heaven (Rev. 5:11, 12). But He never ceases to be the Crucified. He carries "the marks of slaughter upon him" (verse 6, NEB).

Look at His hands and feet. See the wounds from the cross. Christ appears in heaven: real, scarred by the cross, alive, powerful. The One who ate food in the disciples' presence (Luke 24:41-43), who understood their terror (verses 38, 39) and fear about the future—this One goes with us on the mission He commands.

> No more we doubt Thee, glorious Prince of life!
> Life is nought without Thee; aid us in our strife;
> Make us more than conquerors, through Thy
>   deathless love;
> Bring us safe through Jordan to Thy home above.
> Thine is the glory, risen, conquering Son;
> Endless is the victory Thou o'er death hast won.[5]

The final conviction came not from sight, hearing, taste, or touch, but from the Word. Thus two times in Luke 24 the Lord referred to the witness of the Written Word (verses 25-27; 44-47). Overwhelmed by their senses, the disciples might have felt that they had had enough evidence. But Christ did not.

Three and a half years before, Jesus had come out of the wilderness "armed with the power of the Spirit" (Luke 4:14, NEB). Now the same Power would arm His followers (Luke 24:49). The promise of power from above signaled a new initiative in God's purposes. The faithful would wait and then go in power (verse 49) with a message of repentance and forgiveness (verse 47).

The shepherds, Anna and Simeon, the disciples on the Mount of Transfiguration, the observers at the cross—all have a role as witnesses. Witnesses testified to the empty tomb. The apostles and other followers of Jesus had observed "these things" (verse 48). With witness comes the responsibility to testify.

Witness linked with the power of the Spirit created the church. This continues to sustain and expand the Christian gospel. Many had seen the same things as the disciples, but they did not transform the world. The difference for Jesus' followers was the power of the Spirit.

For Jesus, Jerusalem was on the pathway to heaven (Luke 9:51). Now He left the disciples and went to heaven (Luke 24:51). Such a parting was sweet sorrow. They gazed and gazed after the disappearing form of their beloved Master (Acts 1:10). But it did not leave them in tears. Instead they went back into the city with "great joy" (Luke 24:52). The note of joy that began the Gospel and that sounds again and again throughout the story reached its climax with Jesus' ascension. The Man who came to bring joy (Luke 2:10, 11) had met His promise.

Jesus began His ministry in the power of the Holy Spirit (Luke 4:14). As He was about to depart He continued with that Presence (Acts 1:2). Day after day for 40 days He met with the disciples and instructed them (verse 3). Can you imagine that class? How much information can you impart in nearly six weeks? Especially with the help of the

Spirit? If you wonder at the change in Peter and the others, here is part of the answer.

Do not think for a moment that the Galileans went to their task ignorant fishermen or uninstructed country bumpkins. Not at all. Nor should we despise learning when it has the purpose of witness and fulfillment of God's purposes.

During this period of instruction and waiting they asked many questions. For them a key question was "Wilt thou at this time restore again the kingdom to Israel?" (verse 6). Because it had not happened before the Resurrection, would it now? Jesus' answer still instructs us today: Let the Father set the time for the kingdom; you be about the business of witnessing (verses 7, 8).

In the upper room the disciples prayed (verses 13, 14). They did not have to wait long for the coming of the Holy Spirit.

We leave them there, in devotion and prayer in the upper room, as we remember the devout Zacharias who began the Gospel with his prayer, remember the answer given him through the power of the Spirit and in the ministry of angels. Once more we remember Bethlehem, the shepherds, the heavenly chorus.

The formula for God's new beginnings did not change. A purpose to be fulfilled, devout, praying people, the descent of the Holy Spirit, the gifts of heaven—put them together and God sets about His mission.

"For Luke, history was saving only in that it was part of the one history of salvation known to the people of God, the history of Israel. Luke wrote about pious Jews confident in a God that keeps His word. Though life brings surprises—like the inclusion of the Gentiles, the rejection of Israel's leaders, and the destruction of Jerusalem—it still remains the arena for accomplishing God's purposes and for demonstrating His faithfulness." [6]

For God's people His yes is hope. For them His yes is

power and joy. In Jesus the prophecies and promises are fulfilled. From the right hand of the Father, Jesus sends the Holy Spirit.

What reassurance! Therefore Christians worship God with great joy, follow Jesus and never falter, witness with courage and enthusiasm. The whole earth awaits the witness to the salvation given in Jesus. The witness is within us. To say yes to Him is to witness.

God does not call the powerful because of their power, or the wealthy because of their wealth. He found His people resources mainly among the outcast and lowly. He loved to eat with them and to feel their eagerness for His word. Not only does this teach us that we can find salvation however humble or sinful we might be, but it also declares to us that we can be effective and mighty witnesses. The witness belongs to you. You are His witness.

"It is in doing Christ's work that the church has the promise of His presence. . . . The very life of the church depends upon her faithfulness in fulfilling the Lord's commission. To neglect this work is surely to invite spiritual feebleness and decay. Where there is no active labor for others, love wanes, and faith grows dim."[7]

"Ye shall be witnesses unto me . . . unto the uttermost part of the earth" (Acts 1:8).

---

[1] *The Desire of Ages*, pp. 790, 793.

[2] Joseph A. Fitzmyer, *The Gospel According to Luke*, p. 1558.

[3] *The Journal of the Reverend John Wesley*, vol. 1, p. 102.

[4] Eduard Schweizer, *The Good News According to Luke*, pp. 373, 374.

[5] Edmond Budry, "Thine Is the Glory," *The SDA Hymnal*, No. 171. Words from *Cantate Domino*. Copyright by World Student Christian Federation.

[6] Donald Juel, *Luke-Acts: The Promise of History*, pp. 117, 118.

[7] *The Desire of Ages*, p. 825.